Robin David is a journalist, working as assistant editor with the *Times of India*'s Ahmedabad edition. He has extensively covered the Gujarat earthquake of 2001 and the Godhra riots of 2002. He belongs to the small Bene Israel Jewish community of Ahmedabad. *City of Fear* is his first book.

PENGUIN BOOKS

LID OF FEAR

City of Fear

ROBIN DAVID

PENGUIN BOOKS

PENGUIN BOOKS
Published by the Penguin Group
Penguin Books India Pvt. Ltd, 11 Community Centre, Panchsheel Park,
New Delhi 110 017, India
Penguin Group (USA) Inc., 375 Hudson Street, New York, New York 10014, USA
Penguin Group (Canada), 90 Eglinton Avenue East, Suite 700, Toronto,
Ontario, M4P 2Y3, Canada (a division of Pearson Penguin Canada Inc.)
Penguin Books Ltd, 80 Strand, London WC2R 0RL, England
Penguin Ireland, 25 St Stephen's Green, Dublin 2, Ireland (a division of Penguin Books Ltd)
Penguin Group (Australia), 250 Camberwell Road, Camberwell, Victoria 3124, Australia (a division of Pearson Australia Group Pty Ltd)
Penguin Group (NZ), cnr Airborne and Rosedale Roads, Albany, Auckland 1310, New Zealand (a division of Pearson New Zealand Ltd)
Penguin Group (South Africa) (Pty) Ltd, 24 Sturdee Avenue, Rosebank, Johannesburg 2196, South Africa

Penguin Books Ltd, Registered Offices: 80 Strand, London WC2R 0RL, England

First published by Penguin Books India 2007

Copyright © Robin David 2007

All rights reserved

10 9 8 7 6 5 4 3 2 1

ISBN-13: 978-0-14310-137-6   ISBN-10: 0-14310-137-4

The views and opinions expressed in this book are the author's own and the facts are as reported by him which have been verified to the extent possible, and the publishers are not in any way liable for the same. Names of some people have been changed to protect their privacy.

Typeset in Sabon by R. Ajith Kumar, New Delhi
Printed at Presstech Lithographers Pvt. Ltd, Greater Noida

This book is sold subject to the condition that it shall not, by way of trade or otherwise, be lent, resold, hired out, or otherwise circulated without the publisher's prior written consent in any form of binding or cover other than that in which it is published and without a similar condition including this condition being imposed on the subsequent purchaser and without limiting the rights under copyright reserved above, no part of this publication may be reproduced, stored in or introduced into a retrieval system, or transmitted in any form or by any means (electronic, mechanical, photocopying, recording or otherwise), without the prior written permission of both the copyright owner and the above-mentioned publisher of this book.

To Ora

CHAPTER ONE

In the last thirty years, I have come close to dying four times. The first three instances occurred with a distance of ten years between them. The first two were quick, staccato moments, with death staring at me only briefly. Like two individuals in their cars racing down opposite lanes on a highway, stealing glances as they cross each other. And then, surveying the little dot speeding backwards in the rear-view mirror, wondering if that face was familiar.

The last two instances were different. They made death stare at me again and again over long periods of time, and within a year of each other, leaving me with one haunting question I have never been able to answer. Exactly what did Octavio Paz mean when he said, 'We are condemned to kill time, so we die little by little'?

I have always felt that there are many near-death instances waiting for me on this tall spiral of days. But they are meant to be spread over a long stretch of time, appearing at unexpected corners, giving me enough time to sidestep them, to let them fall into the bottomless pit of my past. And in that sense I die little by little, until that one instance which will finally succeed in pouncing on me.

But, since the last two instances, I have been left with this distinct feeling that all those near-death instances, meant to wait for me in my future, have sought me out and accumulated like an unshakeable burden on my shoulders, waiting for the right moment to slit my throat. As if I have not been condemned to kill time, but time has sentenced me to death.

Both of the last two instances I have scanned thoroughly but not found an answer to Paz. So I have gone back to the first two, sieved them out of a clutter of memories and sharpened them as best as hindsight can. Perhaps they hold some answers, omens.

It all began when, as a ten-year-old child, I slipped over a lump of fresh brown-and-black dog shit in the backyard of my home sprinkled with dry bougainvillea flowers. I fell backwards, my spine crashing into the blunt corner of a small cement birdbath. As I got up I realized something was wrong with my breathing. I could only exhale, not inhale. The few drops of air caught in my lungs went out as quickly as the frightened sparrows, which flew away in panic.

I tried to bring back the rhythmic breathing, but it was not working. It felt as if a steel plate was lodged just below my throat from shoulder-tip to shoulder-tip with no vents in between. I was choking. Dying. I rushed into the house. My lungs were about to burst and break through my ribs without their regular supply of air. 'Amrit . . .' I cried out to my sister, but could not finish her name. She was sitting curled up in her usual place by the window in the living room, on the Freudian couch reading one of the many animal books in the house. She saw me, rushed towards me and started rubbing my chest. 'Breathe!' she cried.

Dada, my grandfather with his perfectly trimmed, white handlebar moustache, rushed in and switched on the old ceiling fan, which rattled to the same rhythm as my disappeared breathing. 'What happened?' he asked in his electro-larynx voice. His voice box had been removed after a cancer operation. The machine never allowed him to express surprise, giving out a singular monotone no matter how shocked he may be. The electric voice, the rattling fan, my sister screaming, they created a sensation of life being squeezed out of my body. Slowly.

Was that a cloud of dust mushrooming out of my ears? Was that life? Was that all there was to life? A cloud of dust that can be squeezed out of the ears?

From between a curtain of electric sounds and mushrooming dust, I could see my gravestone in marble in the overcrowded Jewish graveyard of old Ahmedabad: 'Our brave and beloved son, who was killed by a lump of fresh dog shit.'

In a flash, the steel plate melted away. A strong gush of wind rushed in to fill my lungs. I was breathing again. In the garden, where I had fallen, I noticed that my sweaty body had drawn an outline of itself—crooked and uneven—on the dusty garden floor.

Ten years later I was in Israel. I had left my studies halfway after one year of college and a possible bachelor's degree in economics, and packed my bags for Israel. 'Every Jew has the right to immigrate to this country,' the Law of Return said and, at least on paper, ended 2000 years of nationless wanderings of the Jewish people. I decided to test this law one last time and try to end my family's wanderings (which had tried to immigrate to the Promised Land twice before but returned empty-handed and disillusioned).

I landed up in a kibbutz hidden in the foothills of the Galilee, learning Hebrew on an Ulpan programme, washing dishes in the kitchen, listening to stories of how Saddam Hussein's Scuds never killed anyone the year before, attending Friday evening Shabbat prayers regularly for the first time in my life, picking pears in the orchards and weeding wild plants from fragrant oregano fields.

When I think of Israel today, what immediately comes to mind is not the Western Wall, or the golden dome of the Al Aqsa Mosque or the golden skin of Israeli women on Tel Aviv's white beaches. When I think of Israel I think of picking pears. We would start before dawn every morning. A bumpy tractor ride would bring us to an open field surrounded by the dark, ominous shapes of the pear trees. The stars would still be embroidered to the black satin sky when the devout kibbutzniks lit up their prayer books with electric torches and swayed in the darkness as they said their morning prayers. I would fidget, unable to understand the Hebrew.

And then slowly, as if the prayers were being answered, a dark-red glow would appear on the eastern horizon. It would transform into a large, pink palm, which would gently push aside the stars and reveal the true nature of things around us. The pear trees laden with fruit which caught fire but did not burn with the first rays of the sun. The sliced bark of a tree as a breakfast table laden with fresh bread, jugs of coffee, boiled eggs and tinned tuna. The red tractor trolleys. The sharp-nosed, high-cheek-boned kibbutzniks in blue workclothes, their faces glowing as if they were angels. And then a wave of blue would start rolling into the sky. So blue that it would blind me for a brief moment and then I would get used to it.

'You don't have to pull at the fruit,' I was told by a small, bony kibbutznik farmer with a gruff voice better suited to a man much larger than him. Not certain that I had fully understood the first principle of the fine art of picking pears, he took me to a tree with its pears still hanging and added holding one in his hand, 'You have to hold it gently and twist it round till it separates from the branch with the stalk intact. Like this.' He held the light-green bulb in front of my face, a small piece of the stalk still stuck to it, and said, 'If the stalk breaks, the fruit will rot. And rot all other fruit in the container with it.' His words had made more sense than the Heckscher-Ohlin Theory of Foreign Trade, on whose complex graph of thin lines bursting out from the point where the X axis met the Y axis I could never see goods passing the boundaries of nations while sitting in a classroom of seventy students in Ahmedabad.

Then one day the kibbutzniks decided to go trekking into the Galilee. Myth and wind had made the rock smooth. Too slippery for my hemiplegic right foot to hold on to. Death was just a cliff away, three hundred feet down.

But the girl from Hungary with sumptuous breasts, Tziporah, who was part of the Ulpan programme, had already covered twice the distance as if she were a mountain goat. I had to catch up. I had to prove that hemiplegic Indians could climb a mountain too. Any mountain.

To get to the pool of freezing green water, the source of the Sea of Galilee, I had to cross a corner on a cliff at a sharp turn. There was about one foot of flat rock on the other side of the blind curve for a foothold and nothing to get a grip with my hands, except some more smooth, slippery, time-beaten rock.

Tziporah and her sumptuous breasts had to be caught up with. I put my left foot on the other side of the cliff. Only then did I realize the extent of the empty void between the mountain and me. The mountain was real. The void was real. I could die. The void could swallow me.

A tremor ran down the muscles of my hemiplegic right thigh. My right foot slipped a fraction of an inch. And then my left thigh trembled. A bead of sweat slithered on to my spectacles.

The sun was burning down the back of my neck. I could feel the weak muscle-less fingers of my right hand gnawing at the rock, but it refused to turn itself into soft flesh for me to grip it.

And then my right knee buckled. From the corner of my left eye, dry branches of a tree below were visible. If I fell, those dry branches pointing upwards could easily impale me. My body would hang there like a dirty, bloody rag before the kibbutzniks got to the foot of the mountain and picked up my remains. It would be a slow death, with enough time to look up and see half the tree branch jutting out of my stomach. Suddenly I was too afraid to cross over to the other side of the mountain. I was transfixed, standing crucified between the rock and the void and unable to move. If I moved, I would fall. I was certain. I had to prolong the fall. And prolong death.

I turned my head round to single out the tree most likely to impale me. I saw a peacock feather instead. A single multicoloured feather from the tail of a peacock with its thin, white spine, its sea-green eye framed by a metallic brown ring floating down gently. As if it was defying gravity with grit. I was hallucinating with fear, I thought. And then everything was a blur. Voices were throbbing in my brain saying, *Not like this, not like this*, when someone grabbed my wrist and pulled me on to the other side.

I could have sworn I had stood crucified on the two corners of the cliff for a very long while. The kibbutzniks who climbed the mountain with me tell me it was not more than a few seconds. But for me those brief moments will always be standing at the execution of all my unfulfilled desires. 'I am a twenty-year-old virgin. I am not going to die a virgin.' These were the thoughts that floated in my head during those five minutes of a fraction of a second.

As it happened, Tziporah did not fall in love with me for climbing up to the source of the Sea of Galilee. Only the Australian in the trek, Yakov Wolf, had a word of praise. 'You have balls of steel, man,' he said. I am still not sure if that was a compliment. Would he have wondered about the strength of my balls had I not suffered from hemiplegia on the right side of my body? But I slept well that night thinking about climbing Tziporah's smooth, mountain-like breasts.

The mystery of the floating peacock feather remained until many years later when I woke up from deep sleep one morning, startled and awash with sweat. A dream had just recurred. It was one of the only two dreams I have ever remembered. The rest have all been lost to the mist of bad memory. This one was about freefalling from the second-storey terrace of my house, but never hitting the fading blood-red concrete flooring in the garden at the same speed. Moments before crash-landing, my body would start floating down gently like a plucked peacock feather in still air, strongly protesting against gravity. As a child this dream recurred at regular intervals. Each time I would be falling from the second storey; each time I would panic. And then, just as I was about to crash-land into a mangled mass of broken bones and blood, the laws of the peacock feather would take over and I would start defying gravity.

Like magic, there would be a thousand peacock feathers floating down and I would be one of them. My only regret was that the gravitational laws of the peacock feather always took over only a couple of metres from the floor, giving me only brief seconds of floating pleasure. First it was that split second of terror and then three seconds of floating pleasure.

What this peacock feather was doing, drifting in a void thousands of miles away from where peacocks live and dance in the rain, I had never understood initially. It took me some years to realize where the peacock feather had come from. Maybe I carry it inside me at all times. There are times when I want to believe it was this peacock feather that saved me— when the earthquake struck and when bloodthirsty mobs surrounded me.

The other dream is of being unable to scream despite standing face to face with an intruder in my house. As if a white pillow were pressed against my mouth. The scream turns into an echo in my stomach. Intruders have mockingly smiled at my effort to scream.

I admit there are times when I feel that many dreams float inside my head as I sleep. They must be my glittering, multicoloured fish hiding in the coral reef of unfulfilled desire, coming up for fodder each time wakefulness glides away. Or that is what I think happens as I sleep, because, frankly, I don't know.

It is also possible that I don't dream any more, except for the two that keep recurring. Perhaps I am the only man in the world who has dreamless sleep. Perhaps it is as white as the pillow that pushed my scream into my stomach and turned it into an echo.

I have often wondered how it would be to be asleep and yet fully conscious. Because that seems to be the only way to find out if I dream and document them in detail. That would be one way of finding out where they come from and where they go. But for that I have to break down this gate called sleep, which invariably shuts out the other side. There has to be a way of making sleep and wakefulness one. I have tried to make the transition to sleep as slow as possible, hoping to somehow stand half on the side of sleep and half on the side of wakefulness. But it never works . . .

Perhaps it is for the best. Because my invisible dream could also be my worst nightmare.

CHAPTER TWO

On 27 January 2001 the *Times of India*, Ahmedabad carried a report titled 'Gujarat Shakes Up on Republic Day, Bhuj Snaps off Link' by Anil Pathak and Leena Misra. The ghastly details were as follows:

> The state had been hit by what was thought to be the severest earthquake in a century, measuring 7.9 on the Richter scale. In the wake of the tremors that started at 8.40 a.m. and went on for three to four minutes at least 700 people were killed and 2000 injured. The death toll was 250 in Ahmedabad, 150 in Bhuj, 54 in Surendranagar and 27 in Surat. Army battalions had been rushed to Bhuj, the epicentre, for rescue operations.
>
> Other badly affected districts were Rajkot, Jamnagar, Bhavnagar and Surat. Vadnagar and Visnagar in Mehsana district, close to the state capital Gandhinagar, were badly damaged.
>
> In Ahmedabad, seventy buildings collapsed, especially in the Maninagar, Satellite and Ambawadi areas, ten of these caving in up to the second floor. Buildings collapsed in Bhuj, Surat and Navsari too. Eighteen

people were crushed in a stampede. Others died when they jumped off their high-rise apartments. There was a mass exodus from the cities as people fled to safer avenues with their money and valuables.

The telephone lines were disrupted and a power shutdown threw the state completely off-gear.

The government, geared up for the Republic Day celebrations, took time to rush to the aid of the people. The police, who arrived an hour after the quake struck, seemed aghast and helpless in the wake of the disaster, forcing spectators to take over the rescue operations. It was even difficult to operate the bulldozers at some sites where buildings were standing precariously.

Hospitals too were ill-equipped to handle the disaster. Some were forced to administer emergency in the open.

While buildings caved in and roads tilted to one side, the bridges survived the disaster, although the Nehru Bridge and some others developed deep crevices. The Shaking Minarets, the famous fifteenth-century monument of Gomtipur, collapsed with the impact.

Several weddings, lined up for 26 January, an auspicious day, were abandoned in haste. In the Rudralaya apartment in Maninagar, twenty-five people were feared trapped under the collapsed building. Some of those trapped were relatives who had come for a wedding. Outside the rubble, people were seen wailing for their near and dear ones trapped inside.

Chief Minister Keshubhai Patel had promised a compensation of five crore rupees each to Ahmedabad and Bhuj.

Ten years had passed since the Law of Return had failed me. Or I had failed the Law of Return. I don't know which is closer to the truth. What I do know as truth is that I had felt more like a wandering Jew in Israel, out of place at Ashkenazi synagogues at Shabbat prayers despite wearing a white shirt and a crocheted skullcap, never totally mastering Hebrew, and wondering if I wanted to spend the rest of my life picking pears, avocados and carrots. Within a year I had realized that the Promised Land was not my country. Even the strong fragrance of spices, wafting in from the Arab market through the yellowing Jerusalem sandstone, did not help. Just like Teen Darwaza, but not like home.

I confess I liked watching Jerusalem glow in the warm evening Mediterranean sun. The sun burnt black shadows of the ancient buildings into the rough texture of the cobbled streets. As a man, I had filled my lungs with the fragrance of ancient time. As a Jew, I carried an unexplained guilt of not caring for Israel. Of course there was the guilt of adding to the burden of the family by failing to create my own success story in the land where all immigrants had a rags-to-riches tale to tell. But it was better to add to that burden than not accept that the Promised Land was not *our* Promised Land.

Back in Ahmedabad, I thought I would perhaps fit into the closely knit minuscule minority of Bene Israel Indian Jews, who swayed to Hebrew prayers they did not understand. After all I had by then spent a year in and out of orthodox synagogues and picked up enough Hebrew to get the gist of the prayers. I was wrong. Nothing helped. Not the neatly crocheted skullcap I had got back from the Holy Land or even the tsitsit or prayer shawl with its beautiful blue-striped borders I had bought from a shop in the small town of Beit Shaan in the Jordan Valley. The shawl never sat snugly on my shoulders. Perhaps because it is only meant for men who have completed their bar mitzvah.

At the Ahmedabad synagogue I had slunk behind the thin curtain of praying men, closely following their every movement. I had stood up when they stood up and said Shema Yisrael by pinching the bridge of my nose when they did. I could tell that they could tell that I was merely imitating them. What they could not tell was that I was mocking them inside my head for bending from the knees without ever questioning its meaning. It was not long before I stopped going to the synagogue and sleeping in on holidays instead.

On one such perfectly slow wintry morning, I was sleeping, with a framed degree in economics and a job as a newspaper reporter. Israel was a misty memory of blurred faces and clarinet-soaked klezmer music in the backdrop of the bluest skies, and the shapely bronzed legs of Sabra women I was never able to touch. Nothing triggered these memories better than the fragrance of oregano from my days of weeding wild plants in oregano fields. But that was only once in a while.

I was wondering if I had the courage to leave the warmth of my quilt as I woke up, my eyes still misty with sleep. Outside the window closest to my bed on the south side of the house, sparrows fluttered among bougainvillea flowers. A view that almost never changed. The bougainvillea creeper with its delicate blood-red flowers entwined with the bark of the robust neem tree like two lovers in a tight embrace. The tall eucalyptus tree, with its slim, white bark, stood erect next to them, indifferent to the love embrace, and the sparrows flitted around like wild gypsy children.

The wire mesh on the window, meant to keep mosquitoes out of the house, provided the thick, rough texture for this painting. The bougainvilleas were the blobs of brightness in a canvas where the clear blue sky of wintry mornings burst out from a network of green leaves and thin, brown branches. Completing the picture was the white streak running off-centre at the left of the frame from top to bottom. That was the eucalyptus bark. I could never see the nest of leaves at the top, just the mid-section of the bark.

Even the strongest breeze could not change this view. It could at best make the eucalyptus sway a little to remove it from the frame of the window. As if someone had taken an eraser and rubbed it off in a single stroke. But that was only for a brief moment. Soon it would swing back into position and complete the view.

Once in a while, when thick early morning sleep overpowered me, this view would dissolve into a large blob of many indistinguishable colours. The blood red of the bougainvillea would flow into the green of the leaves and into the blue of the sky. The streak of white would turn into a flowing river, zigzagging and breaking the banks. It was one of those mornings.

The sounds of my family climbed up the eucalyptus tree and wafted in from the kitchen exactly below my room. My sister, who after many journeys met Nathaniel, her French husband, in a kibbutz in Israel, had come down from France for a holiday with their six-month-old son, Kiran. The ruffling of newspapers by Nathaniel, the clanking of pots by mother preparing to make strong tea with milk and fresh mint, the unintelligible squeaks of my nephew, the thought of the glow of reflected sunlight filtering through the dense neem tree to fall on the breakfast table around which my family sat in a semi-circle—together they seemed to say it was time to wake up.

But then the quilt was warm in contrast to the cool wind from the window and it was a rare holiday after all. It was Republic Day, a day when you could afford to sleep in late. A few years earlier I would have woken up early especially on Republic Day to watch the armed forces parade at the Red Fort on television. As a boy I had loved the sight of the tanks and their gleaming barrels, the spanking uniforms of the soldiers, the helicopters showering rose petals. And then I would switch off the television as soon as the prime minister started his annual speech on the state of the nation.

In 2001, however, I decided to sleep in and practise my favourite game of standing half on the side of sleep and half on the side of wakefulness. It was on days like these that I strongly felt there had to be a way of breaking the sleep barrier and yet remaining asleep.

The heavy paperweights of sleep were starting to dangle on my eyelids. I was floating now. Gently. The warmth of the quilt was enveloping me. I was reaching it. The state. I was there. Half asleep and half awake. I think. Because I could have been sleeping and dreaming about being awake. I was not sure. But it was perfect Republic Day sleep. Or wakefulness. Sucking me in. Every muscle in my body was succumbing to the state. As if the muscles had lost their grip on the bones they had clung on to for so long. As if they had turned to liquid and started floating inside my body. Like jelly. My whole body had become jelly, floating, gliding, rocking a little.

Suddenly the rocking turned violent. It was more than the slow trembling of jelly. Something was wrong. I was not rocking. My bed was. Something had rumbled and I was not sure where, under the bed or in the sky. And it was still rumbling. Rolling like thunder.

But it was not rolling like thunder. Monsoon clouds never gathered in the Ahmedabad sky in January. Could have been a jet plane, perhaps. But the rumble was too close and went on for too long. Even the langurs that attacked our garden once every fortnight did not make so much noise. It would take a stampede by a thousand langurs to create this rumble.

Something was wrong but I could not tell what. My bed was rocking like an old, wooden boat in a choppy sea. I held on to the sides and looked around. The ancient, seven-feet-tall Godrej almirahs, which otherwise needed the effort of two burly men to be moved, had now become belly dancers, gyrating towards the centre of the room on their own. The old Bombay fornicator chair with its large, out of proportion handrests too was walking towards me from the other end of the room.

The only piece of furniture not walking towards me was the heavy-set steel table at the right-hand side of the room. Its three drawers opened by themselves. My past started tumbling out of them. Forgotten photographs of forgotten girlfriends, childhood drawings in black ink of the network of dry tree branches, an acupressure ball, a decade-old Hebrew–English dictionary, a textbook of Keynesian economics I had never opened . . . There were too many things. The loudest was the small Y-shaped tuning fork for the guitar, which danced on the floor for a few brief moments, giving out a clear A note from between the muffled thuds of falling books and photographs, before settling down with the rest of the things on the floor.

All this happened in a matter of a few seconds. Then I suddenly caught sight of my favourite window from the corner of my right eye. It was shaking like a rubbery yo-yo. Up and down. Left and right. Windows did not shake like this. Was I sleeping? Is this what happens when you are caught between sleep and wakefulness? A terrible trembling of the universe? Even without the weight of sleep on my eyelids, the colours outside the window were caught in a wild whirlpool where they merged into a singular undistinguishable mass—the blood red into the green into the blue. The eucalyptus bark was not swinging. It was shivering. I was awake. And the colours were still merging. My bed was not a boat in choppy water. The entire house was a rocking boat and the firm earth below was the choppy sea.

Earthquake.

I was running out, but being pushed back by thick waves under my feet. The current was too strong. I had to wade to the veranda, which led to the staircase going downstairs. I caught a glimpse of my favourite neem tree in the neighbour's garden. A giant more than a hundred feet tall and with a thousand arms to support colonies of birds, it was trembling like a witch doctor who had fallen into a trance after taking just the right dose of opium. Its pointed little green leaves used to flutter in the sunset-drenched breeze of summer evenings. But this was not evening and there was not the slightest sign of wind. And yet the leaves were fluttering.

Everything was fluttering. The staircase was swinging as if it was a tightrope held up by jittery springs, not wooden poles.

Mother was standing at the bottom of the staircase. 'What's going on,' she asked almost casually, her eyebrows only gently arched with concern. 'Earthquake!' I screamed, holding on to the railing on the right for balance. 'Out! Get out!' Being on the ground floor, they had not felt the full force of the choppy sea of the earth.

'Out!' my mother started shouting. 'Amrita out! Nathaniel out!' She was holding on to the door with all her strength as if she were Samson and would have taken the entire weight of the two-storey house on her shoulders if it crumbled before her family ran out.

Within the next few moments we were standing on the dusty road outside the house. Dazed. 'What happened?' my sister asked. 'Don't know,' I said. 'Not sure. Has to be some kind of earthquake.' By then the choppy sea had turned tranquil. The earth had fallen silent. 'How long do you think it lasted?' I asked looking at Nathaniel. 'More than a minute, I think,' he said. 'Not sure.'

We stood around for a while not knowing what to do next. There was quietude everywhere. The neighbours had run out of their homes. Autorickshaws and scooters were plying on the main road. There were some people running around, but nothing really seemed out of place.

'It's over, I think,' I ventured. How was I to know that earthquakes are never fleeting? They can make room for themselves in your memory and last forever.

For the moment everything seemed to be returning to normal. Something had grabbed our homes, shaken them violently and then let go. Our homes were standing but something was not right. Something was missing. Everything was silent, and yet it was not peaceful. As if the body was alive, but the pulse was missing. I started looking for the pulse.

I first looked for it in the neem tree next door. Older than our house, its strongest branches always sang paeans to life, humming with sounds of crows squabbling over dead rats, clusters of green parrots hiding in the leaves, calling out to each other, giving the impression that the tree had a voice of its own.

Disturbed by the squirrels, a party of parrots would burst out in a cloud of green from behind the leaves, as if a part of the tree itself was flying away. Amidst all this lived the bee-eaters, the kingfishers, the robins, the sunbirds which stood motionless in mid-air over delicate flowers, the rosy pastors, the tailorbirds, the bulbuls, a blue jay, a golden oriole and a crow pheasant with eyes more red than bougainvillea flowers. And then of course there was the black ibis couple, perched right at the top of this buzzing universe, looking at everything, as if with complete detachment.

But now, none of it was there. The tree was there, green and standing, but the universe had fallen silent. The crows, the doves, the parrots, the ibises were missing. Only the squirrels were fluttering around, giving out their short, staccato calls of panic. The tree was alive only by its colour. The rest of life seemed to have flown away.

Inside my room the almirahs had to be pushed back against the walls. Things from the drawers had to be picked up from the floor. The only reassuring aspect was the window. It had stopped swinging and brought to an end the swirling whirlpool of colour. The demarcations had returned. The straight white line, the blood-red blobs of brightness and the green backdrop punctuated by bursts of bright-blue holes.

And yet, something was missing. The sparrows had flown away. So had the gentle breeze. Without them, the painting was just a dull picture postcard. It was too silent.

I considered getting back into the warmth of the quilt, but sleep had already evaporated. Instead, I started picking up the many objects scattered on the floor. The first thing to come into my hand was a photo album with photos of my first girlfriend, Venessa, an American bisexual I had met in Israel ten years ago. Our relationship had not even lasted six months, but in a moment of affection she had presented me the album on my twenty-second birthday. It contained faded snapshots of her twenty-three-year journey, from a smiling infant to a tomboyish teenager to an extremely thin, pretty woman with dark-blue eyes. The album should have gone out of the house the day Venessa called up from Staten Island, New York to say, 'Robin, I don't think this long-distance thing is going to last.' I had tried to play the perfect gentleman and posted the album back to her, but it was returned undelivered with a sticker on the envelope claiming that no one by the name of Venessa Katz lived at that address. And then for the last ten years it had remained locked up in the drawer opened only by the earthquake.

There was also the notebook in which I had practised my Hebrew letters a decade ago. The pencil marks had faded. I could not tell a 'khet' from a 'zine', or if the three dots underneath a letter meant the vowel *e* or the vowel *u*.

There were love letters from Manali, another girlfriend I had met in college after coming back from Israel. She was now married. I could not stand the mushy, perfectly rhymed verse in Hindi. These too should have seen the bottom of a garbage bin a long time ago.

There were other objects on the floor I did not even know still existed. Like the guitar strings, coiled and rusted. I could not remember when I bought them, or the last time I had broken a string on the guitar. Or the last time I had strummed the guitar.

The largest chunk of my childhood lying on the floor was drawings in black ink of large dry trees. There was no play of light and shade. Just a network of ad hoc thin lines from a large block of black meant to signify a trunk. They looked like silhouettes, without texture, without contours. The sun was a large circle, half hidden behind the network. At other times the sun would be replaced with a minaret, a balcony and a dome. Or a plane would fly by again hidden behind the network. In this pile of black ink, there were only a handful of men either standing or resting their shoulders on the bark or sitting underneath the network playing a flute. Always a silhouette. In black ink. The network looked more like cracks on a wall than the branches of a tree.

I had lost the desire to paint many years ago and should have thrown the drawings out much before the trembling started. But then there was so much that I should have disposed of.

I stood up. If I rummaged any further, I would come across more unfinished tasks. Many things and people had walked out of my life leaving behind only symbolic gestures and reminders. The thin layer of dust which had settled on the objects over the years lifted and tingled my nostrils.

I started dumping everything back into the drawers as quickly as possible. But it was not easy. Over the years, these objects had created room for themselves in the drawers. They had settled in and managed to find a specific place for themselves so that the drawers closed comfortably. The drawings were at the base. The Hebrew notebooks rested on them with the photographs, the acupressure ball, the guitar strings, the tuning fork, the little boxes with stones and seashells, the economics textbooks, the love letters . . .

But now they bulged out and it seemed impossible to fit them back again. As if the drawers had suddenly shrunk. As if it was magic that so many objects had found a place in such little space. Only the drawings had settled down. For the rest there was no room. It was irritating. I started pushing even harder. In the unnatural silence, without the wind and the sparrows, the sound of rusted metal drawers rubbing against each other gave me goose pimples.

I gave up.

I started looking around the room and caught sight of a hairline crack, running from the corner of the window sill on the right side into the corner where the walls met. The house was old and age had brought out many cracks, but this one was new. There were new cracks everywhere. At other window sills, near the door, at the corners where the walls met. Was it possible that these cracks had always existed and I was noticing them only now?

It was then that I noticed the old crack running across the room on all the four walls exactly two feet below the ceiling. This was an old and obstinate crack. When Dada was alive, he had made numerous attempts to have it removed. He would order the masons to remove five inches of plaster on either side of the crack and go right down to the red bricks, to fill it again with fresh plaster and have the entire wall whitewashed. Proudly, he would survey the wall for the next few days, as if it was his work of art.

And then slowly, a thin, black line would reappear above my favourite window as if it were yawning and waking up from deep sleep. Then it would start running a marathon and cover the rest of the room. Every day it would cover some ground, like scissors cutting into the plaster. Patiently.

Dada's eyes would chase the crack every day, first with a little irritation and then with dejection as it ran all the way across the room and met itself over the window. Resurrection would be complete.

This time, however, it seemed to have opened up on its own without help from Dada, who had been buried in the Jewish graveyard for more than ten years. It seemed as if the crack had separated the roof from the rest of the wall. As if the house had a lid which could be opened and closed.

CHAPTER THREE

At a distance, on the Guptanagar main road, cries started to ring through. People calling out to each other in voices overflowing with panic. The voices started trickling closer and closer to the house, first in thin lines. Then there was a loud burst of sound everywhere. A crescendo of human voices was building up, but there was no meaning in them. Just voices, trying to tell me that something terrible had happened. They only brushed against my senses, but even in that slight touch, the trembling, the shaking was obvious. Wave after wave followed. You had to listen very carefully to pick up the singular lines of words, of meaning, threading themselves on the weave of sound. Of chaos.

I ran out only to be caught up in the terrible cyclone of sounds. 'You know Rameshbhai the richshawalla? His wife started running out of the house when the earth began to tremble . . . A wall fell on her. Died on the spot. Her five-year-old daughter was with her. She died too.' The son? 'He didn't run. He lived.' And Rameshbhai? 'He wasn't at home.'

I ran to the slum at the back of the house. The entrance, I knew, was narrow with very thin walls of exposed red brick on both sides. There was very little cement between the bricks.

Jamna's body could be made out from underneath the torn blanket used to cover her. Beside her lay a lump a couple of feet away. That was her daughter. The two bodies were at the mouth of the entrance. Just two more steps and they would have made it into the open, away from the collapsing wall. But they were swallowed by the narrowness of the entrance and the thinness of the wall. Their bodies lay in total silence. Still. Confirming that nothing would ever shake them again.

In this stillness, another wave of sound started to build up, first in a meaningless buzz of the voices of a thousand people shouting at the same time and then constructing itself into coherence. Another building had fallen, two kilometres away from the largest Muslim ghetto of India called Juhapura, outside the city limits of Ahmedabad.

The four-storeyed Akbar Apartments looked as if a giant sledgehammer had hit it in the centre of the roof. And the thin pillars it stood on had collapsed so that all that was left was a chaotic heap. Men climbed over the rubble, removing large slabs of concrete with their bare hands. They could hear faint cries from within the heap, as if the trapped people were right underneath, making the men at the top even more frantic in their search. But the voices remained distant even after bruised hands had removed layer after layer of concrete.

The search went on. Until suddenly the concrete caved in even further like a large slab of ice melting in the hot afternoon sun. The cries stopped. Silence returned all over again. The men scrambled down from the collapsing rubble as quickly as they could, fearing for their lives. Everyone else watched.

First in total silence and then with howls of horror as it dawned upon them that they had just been witness to an execution by nature.

The cries started becoming louder. Women, hidden behind black burqas, were screaming for their relatives who were most likely dead. Men in white kurtas and grey beards were beating their chests in between loud sobs. A string of ambulance sirens started to ring as they moved in to pick up the remains. A police van followed. Men in khaki jumped out and started screaming orders to the crowd to stay away from the rubble. The noise reached a crescendo of anguish and despair.

'Execution by nature,' I said to myself in a voice even I could not hear in the rising wall of sound. 'Execution by nature,' I said again, this time a little louder but, like waves in low tide, the words only crashed against the wall of my throat and subsided, never reaching up to my ears.

The receding wave of words filled my chest with fear. I could have been a victim of this execution too, not just a witness. My entire family could have been slaughtered while I was rocking in bed with the first tremors, while the colours fused outside my window, while I watched my past jump out of untouched drawers. At that moment, people elsewhere had looked up to see the roofs of their homes cave in on them; they had seen walls collapse like the pages of a book held up by a delicate hand and released unexpectedly. They had jumped from the swaying fourth-storey balconies and landed to their deaths. They had been cut in two by falling slabs of concrete. Some had spent hours caught in air pockets, hoping that someone would hear their cries for help and then slowly suffocated to death.

'Execution by nature.' I was not saying the words any more and yet I could hear them. Ringing loud and clear inside my head. They were banging against my skull. Each letter was a miniature sledgehammer trying to break free.

By the time I reached home, my throat was parched. My temples were throbbing as if my heart had shifted from my chest to my head. I was wondering how I would even begin to tell the story of what I had seen to my family. How we had escaped the singular blow of the sledgehammer. How we had escaped execution. Death.

But as it turned out, they had much more to tell me. They had seen it all on television. The ocean of movement we had experienced was in fact the biggest earthquake ever. Initial reports showed it measured 7.9 on the Richter scale. Somehow 7.9 seemed too small to describe what we had experienced.

And then the real numbers started trickling in. In the forty-five seconds that the earth turned liquid, more than 700 people died in Ahmedabad alone. Thousands more had died in Kutch, 400 kilometres north of the city in the semi-desert land, where the epicentre was located. While one minister blurted in front of the television cameras that he suspected at least 100,000 to be dead, later reports showed that about 12,000 people were killed that day, dragged to their death in the whirlpool of motion.

Like Akbar Apartments, thirty other buildings had collapsed while I had been studying the blurring of colour outside my window. Bodies had piled up in hospitals and they were running out of shrouds. So the doctors used anything they could lay their hands on. As I would find out later that afternoon while visiting the VS Hospital, in many cases, the pieces of cloth were not big enough to cover the entire body. So body parts jutted out. Toes barely hanging on to the foot, sliced as if with a fresh, sharp knife, but not completely. There were palms with two fingers missing. From under the small bed sheets it was not difficult to make out that there were entire hands and legs missing from many bodies, or even faces smashed to pulp, the sharp contours of noses and cheekbones flattened.

For the first time in thirty years I came to appreciate my distorted hemiplegic body because it was still there. It was all there—the squint in the right eye that I tried to hide by never looking directly into anyone's eyes; the thin, emaciated piece of flesh on the right side of my body called a hand that remained bent inwards from the elbow and had only half the muscles of the left hand, and therefore needed to be hidden behind full-sleeved shirts; and the right foot, which when I was a child would start every step at ninety degrees to the left foot but moving in a semi-circle would become parallel by the end of the step—none of that mattered now.

On the second night after the earthquake, I heard footsteps in the garden in front of the house and rushed out to the balcony to see who it was. A man in a grey chequered shirt and black pants had already scaled the walls of the garden and was trying to find an opening to get inside the house. 'Chor!' I tried to scream, but my voice refused to well up from inside my stomach. I breathed hard and tried again.

'Chor!' But my voice went even deeper into my stomach. As if it had been crushed by the heavy weight of a large, black stone in my chest. Anything below it would remain there forever and never reach my throat to burst out in loud cries and startle the intruder.

Just then the man looked up and saw me. His face was boyish, thin, sunburnt, with thick, square lips and small, beady eyes. He smiled. He must have known of my crushed voice. I filled my lungs with air in the hope of spitting out the black stone and rediscovering my ability to scream and he rushed towards the garden wall to jump over it.

And then I heard my mother scream from a distance somewhere deep inside the house. 'Run!' she was crying. 'Get out, get out! It's coming! It's coming!' Why were all of us running after the intruder? Someone should have been calling the police . . . But within moments the entire family was out of the house once again. Mother, Amrita, Nathaniel, little Kiran and I.

Only then did I realize that I was awake. The intruder was inside my head, my recurring dream. Mother had felt a slight tremor shake her bed and made everyone rush out. But there were no waves of panic outside. The neighbours were sleeping silently, most of them outside their houses, afraid of the possibility of yet another tremor. Stray dogs were sniffing in corners to mark out their territory with urine and the street lamp had drawn a huge yellow circle of light on the empty street.

The problem was with mother's wooden bed. It was old and rickety. When she changed sides, its old legs invariably shook and creaked. For the last ten years, she had slept in the same bed, with the mattress developing a slight depression the size of her body. For the last ten years, it had creaked and shaken a little. And she had slept soundly, the creaks drowned by her occasional snoring. But now, after the earthquake, the same creaks had acquired new meaning. They were making her shudder with fear.

We inspected the house from the outside, and saw two large, black eyes peering at us from behind the garden door. We had forgotten Ora, our white Spitz, in the house and she had not liked it. Normally, when we walked out of the garden door, we disappeared from her eyesight, her universe, for a few hours. This time too we had rushed out of the garden door, but had not disappeared. We stood there and kept surveying the house as if waiting for something to happen. And we never walked out of the house at that hour. The way she kept looking at us, it seemed as if she knew she had been forgotten. She knew she had been left out of something else.

She was confused and I was irritated. 'Mom, from now on, let me decide whether it is a tremor or not,' I said. 'Or we will run out every few minutes.' She did not protest, but went inside and started packing a bag with all the money there was in the house, passports, some clothes, cheque books . . . 'What are you doing now?' I asked a little more irritated. What was she hoping to do with a bag at two in the morning?

'It's my runaway bag. I am not going to run out empty-handed,' she said. Her voice was low and trembling slightly.

'Mom, stop panicking,' I said exasperated. 'Our house has withstood whatever it had to withstand. I don't think you should worry about it now.'

For the first time since morning, she looked straight into my eyes and asked, 'How do you know?' I was speechless. I did not know. 'I can't sleep, Robin,' she went on, the trembling a little more pronounced. 'There are cracks all over the place. There isn't a single wall without them. I can even see them in the dark. Without the lights, Robin.' She was sobbing. I held her in my arms and looked around in the glare of the two tube lights burning in the living room. We were standing underneath a canopy of cracks.

But we lived on under the same canopy, singling out every crack and filling it in one by one. Once in a while when a slight tremor hit the city, we would rush out, panic for a few minutes, but then move back in and start filling the cracks.

Like one evening when I was sitting on the Freudian couch in the living room watching bodies slither out of the water on *Baywatch*, the couch started swinging forwards and backwards gently. 'Ora, stop scratching,' I called out. But Ora appeared from the kitchen with a sheepish look on her face. If Ora was in the kitchen, I was swinging by myself . . . 'Run!' I screamed, and mother and I were standing outside within moments.

By now, my sister and her family were back in France and the two of us had perfected the art of running out at the hint of a tremor. Mother always kept the runaway bag next to the door on the floor and Ora always had a leash fastened to her collar, which trailed her like a second tail, often getting entangled in the furniture. As soon as the shaking began, mother would rush towards the door and the runaway bag, I would rush towards Ora's second tail and we would be out of the house in ten seconds.

Slowly, the frequency of the tremors reduced and Ora's second tail was detached. Then, one day, mother forgot to carry the runaway bag with her to the bedroom, a routine she never missed. Only in the morning, while sipping her large beer mug of hot tea with milk and mint, did she realize that perhaps for the first time in many months she had slept soundly without the bag next to her, and without waking up in the middle of the night to ensure that it was still there. Her occasional snores were starting to drown the creaking of the legs of her old bed. It was a good sign.

CHAPTER FOUR

On 28 February 2002 the *Times of India*, Ahmedabad reported on 'a ghastly incident which has shocked the collective consciousness of the entire nation'. The front-page report by Sajid Shaikh was titled '57 Die in Ghastly Attack on Train: Mob Targets Ram Sevaks Returning from Ayodhya'. The details:

> At least fifty-seven people, including twenty-five women and fourteen children, were burnt alive and over thirty injured when the Ahmedabad-bound Sabarmati Express was pelted with stones and petrol bombs by a mob at Godhra junction.
>
> The incident occurred near Singal Falia, located a couple of hundred metres from the Godhra junction. Apparently, around 7.30 a.m., someone pulled the chain and a mob rushed towards two coaches, S-6 and S-7, pelting stones. Then they threw petrol bombs inside through the broken windows. According to survivors, the mob doused the S-6 coach with petrol and diesel and set it on fire as passengers screamed helplessly.
>
> As many as thirty people were charred to death while several more collapsed as their lungs were filled with

smoke. There were 100 passengers in the coach as against the normal capacity of seventy-five. All of them were Ram Sevaks returning after a two-day stay in Ayodhya. They were reportedly the first batch of Ram Sevaks to go to Ayodhya from Gujarat.

By 11 a.m., the coach was completely burnt, with charred bodies everywhere. About thirty-six persons were rushed to the Godhra Civil Hospital with burn injuries.

Reports on how the incident had happened conflicted one another. One report said that a mob, provoked by fiery speeches inside the mosque at Singal Falia, rushed at the coaches they knew were carrying the VHP activists. As per another report, a rumour that the Ram Sevaks on the train had attacked a mosque in Dahod had triggered off the incident.

An accompanying report said 'Violence Spreads Like Wild Fire in State'. In an outpouring of grief and anger at the attack on the Sabarmati Express people had resorted to violence in Godhra and other towns and cities of Gujarat. Three persons were killed in stabbings and police firing. Curfew was imposed on Godhra and shoot-at-sight orders issued. The VHP has called for a state-wide bandh the next day to protest against the attack on its volunteers. There were reports of mob violence from Vadodara, Anand and Ahmedabad as news of the train attack spread.

■

The Guptanagar house made mother melancholic at dusk. That was the only time of the day when the soft sun burst directly into the house; the rays slit into a thousand shafts by the leaves of the neem trees that surrounded the house. As if the sun itself had been sliced into a thousand glowing pieces. The light would enter from the kitchen window, bounce off the Formica on the dining table, reflect on to the glass cabinets in which we kept our china and fill the entire kitchen with a soft glow.

The rest of the house would be immersed in darkness with only a weak afterglow falling on the Freudian couch from the window in the living room. Because the sunlight was beautiful, we never switched on the tube lights until much later.

When mother stood in front of the kitchen window, the slanting light stretched her elongated shadow from the kitchen floor into the drawing room and up to the front door of the house. Was it just the play of light or was it her shadow, I could never tell, but she felt extremely lonely at that hour. It was what the family called the Six o'clock Syndrome. Her past, peopled by those she had loved and lost and those she hated but was not able to forget, would appear from the dark corners of the house to stand in front of her.

As if the setting sun had chosen to carefully place a heavy ball of disquiet between her chest and stomach. With every inch that the sun dipped, the ball would become larger. The only cure was to rush out of the house and spend an hour in some busy part of the city—like Manek Chowk, Teen Darwaza or Ambawadi—on the pretext of buying the best green tea and fresh mint for the morning, or a bracelet for little Kiran. Rubbing shoulders with a crowd was the best cure for the numerous troublesome memories. Like the fear of being abandoned by her children, the guilt of abandoning her father during her sudden flights to Israel, not having enough money and the sporadic appearances of cobras in the garden during monsoon.

Ask her where she was off to and she would say, 'Just for a chakkar.' She would come back with knick-knacks, which she would talk about happily, forgetting those who hid in the dark corners of the house at dusk.

On 27 February 2002, I was in Vadodara and was certain that not having anyone else in the house would make her run out even earlier. By late afternoon the Sabarmati Express had already left Vadodara and was on its way to Ahmedabad. The first reports of stabbings and arson were trickling in. A couple of stabbings had taken place at the Vadodara railway station itself.

I called mother up.

'Mom, don't go out of the house today,' I said. 'There may be trouble.' Television tickers were already flashing the train burning incident. Our office was flooded with phone calls from people wanting to confirm rumours. I assumed she had already heard of the attack.

She hadn't.

'I wanted to ask you something,' she said, sounding preoccupied, 'Every time I try to write something on the computer, the new line eats up the old line. What is happening? I have an important letter to send. What should I press?'

'Press "insert",' I said.

'Okay, wait,' she said, went away for a few moments, came back and then asked, 'Yeah, it's okay now. What were you saying?'

'I was saying don't let your Six o'clock Syndrome bother you today. Don't go out this evening. We are expecting trouble . . .'

'What trouble?'

'Haven't you heard about the train?'

'What train?'

'Muslims have killed some kar sevaks returning from Ayodhya in a train attack at Godhra this morning. And now the VHP has given a call for a bandh tomorrow . . . There is bound to be some madness.'

'Oh shit . . . How many have they killed?'

'More than fifty, it seems . . .'

'My God! What the hell is going to happen now? Are they bringing the bodies to Ahmedabad?'

'Yes, the train is on its way. Just left Vadodara.'

'This one woman was supposed to come and see me in the afternoon but she said she couldn't come because the train was coming. I had no idea what she was talking about.'

'She was talking about this train. The Sabarmati Express. You can expect the VHP to go berserk right from the station itself. In fact you should fill up the fridge just in case. If it becomes like '92, you will be stuck inside for days. And you will have to deal with the Six o'clock Syndrome from inside the house today.'

'Okay, I'll switch on the tube lights a little earlier.'

The next day I was in Godhra to find out how the police were investigating the burning of the train. The town was silent, shut down by a curfew, but the murmurs of discontent could be heard from behind closed doors, echoing off the walls of the narrow lanes. 'That there . . . that is a sensitive area,' people said. 'That's where Muslims stay. Don't talk to us. If you have the guts go talk to them. Ask them why they are so murderous . . .'

Nothing else was happening, except the odd instance of arson. A Bohra's shoe shop had been set on fire, and a small group of teenagers was preventing a fire engine from getting to the burning shop. The police came in and chased the boys away, making the inner rumblings even louder. It was almost as if the walls of the houses had developed voices of their own. They were standing still and shouting in uncontrollable fits of anger. And I was wondering what I could take back to my office for a story. Small fires in small shops and talking walls were not going to make a big story at a time when even bigger fires were raging all over Gujarat.

That was until I met the head of the Gujarat Anti-Terrorist Squad. A tall, strongly built man, he had decided within twenty-four hours that the attack on the train was the equivalent of a terrorist attack. 'The attack is so ghastly that it can only be meant to strike terror in the hearts of people,' he said, his voice bearing the certitude of a man who had no doubts. He talked about how they were suspecting a foreign hand, that of the Inter-Services Intelligence of Pakistan, in the attack and how the Gujarat police itself had no network of intelligence on the kar sevaks coming back so that they could be provided security while passing through sensitive areas.

He did not know me from Adam but he wanted to speak

and I wanted a story. I also understood that the attack had been branded as a conspiracy against the nation. 'Foreign hand' etc. all pointed in one direction—A Muslim Conspiracy. Gujarat was going to burn and for a long time. There was no need for investigation. The mood had been set.

Our photographer Bharat Pathak and I jumped into the white Tata Sumo taxi we had come in and left for Vadodara.

What we did not expect is that in the eighty kilometres between Godhra and Vadodara there lay a hungry eighty-kilometre-long snake with a thousand heads, ready to devour anything that looked even vaguely Muslim. It crawled slowly but stung with the force of a thousand fangs.

Our first encounter with the snake was in the form of an old blue police van. It broke off from the crawling mass, like a scout sent to test the waters. We parked the taxi on the side of the road and waited. The van came and stood about twenty metres away. A policeman got off from the driver's seat. The only remains of his uniform were the freshly polished shoes sparkling even when covered in dust and the khaki pant and bush shirt with the first four buttons open, showing the white banian inside with red stains. It could have been the red juice of the paan he was chewing that had stained his shirt, or it could have been blood. I could not tell. He had removed the mandatory nameplate and all his stars so that he would not be easily identified. The khaki shirt was dripping with sweat and sticking to his thin frame. Even Bharat, a veteran of many riots, had not seen something like this: a policeman as part of the mob, scouting for the mob, walking towards us with the swagger of the owner of the land, out to collect his due.

Bharat decided to take charge. 'Stay in the car,' he told me. 'Don't come out. And don't open your mouth. They should not know you are not a Gujarati.'

I had to protest. 'But I am a Gujarati,' I said. 'And I speak perfect Gujarati.'

Bharat was in no mood for an argument. 'Do what I say and we'll live,' he said.

I shut up.

Getting out of the taxi, Bharat shouted, 'Jai mataji.' But the policeman was not interested. 'Who are you?' he asked, his voice deadpan, advancing towards us. Slowly. 'Hindus,' Bharat added, 'from the press.'

The words had the desired impact. 'Oh Hindus from the press,' he said, the coldness of his voice replaced with a small degree of respect. 'Okay then. Go ahead.' He waved to the crowd, 'Let them pass brothers, they are one of us.' The mob started parting, exposing the thin strip of broken road expected to take us to Vadodara. To safety.

But the snake was irritated. It was hungry too. It was not going to let us pass easily. The thousand heads with thin torsos started running along the taxi. 'Say it,' they were shouting. 'Jai Shree Ram!' We shouted back with equal vigour. 'Don't forget it's your battle too,' one of the heads added. 'Don't let them get away with this.'

We shouted one more time, 'Jai Shree Ram!'

The running men, their sunburnt bodies doused in sweat and sparkling under the glare of the afternoon sun, looked like the glistening scales of a large cobra. Interwoven into each other and ensuring that the serpent crawled. The clanking of their rusted swords and farm equipment rubbing against the tar on the road sounded like the shaking tail of a large rattlesnake. Angry. Hungry.

As the car moved ahead, the road fell silent between villages. But there were remnants of a violent struggle everywhere. Boulders and large trunks of trees were strewn on the road. Small families were running away from something. Scared by the sound of the taxi, they would sometimes take cover behind bushes by the side of the road.

Someone had grabbed my heart with pliers to create a large pressure bubble at the lower end. And then someone pricked this bubble with a thin sewing needle to let droplets of fear trickle into the already existing lake at the bottom of my stomach. With every drop, the lake was swelling, rising, threatening to drown my heart, my lungs, my throat, me.

Little droplets of fear appeared on Bharat's forehead. Our driver, who had joined in with his observations to our conversations in the morning, was now silent. There was too much silence when Bharat spoke. 'From now on, you will park the car on the side of the road whenever I tell you to,' he told the driver. 'Don't try to run past them. Don't try to ram them. Don't panic. Don't try anything or we'll be finished. The moment you see a mob, wait for my orders and then park the car. The first stone has to be stopped. That is the key. Stop the first stone and you will go home alive. Can't stop it and you will be stoned to death.'

Barely had Bharat finished explaining his theory of the first stone when the second mob appeared on the horizon. This one was much larger and better armed, but disorganized. There was no blue van scouting to make first contact. Every single one of the oily scales was a leader here and they took individual decisions. We could tell from a distance that the men had come out on the streets with anything that could be used as a weapon. There were axes, sickles, dharias, metal pipes, even a small plough.

About 100 metres from the mob, Bharat asked the driver to park the taxi on the side, but he took his own time before veering to the left, inviting Bharat's wrath. 'Bhenchod, park the fucking car NOW!' he barked and the startled driver immediately swerved. Bharat got down. 'Jai Shree Ram,' he called out, but the mob kept gravitating towards us. Only a few answered back, 'Jai Shree Ram.' Others wanted to confirm the facts for themselves. Slowly, they started encircling the taxi, like a large python closing all escape routes around a small prey.

One of them, a thin man with powerful shoulders, rested a small plough on the bonnet of the taxi. Gently, just so that he did not scratch the white paint. Others started sticking their small faces into the glass of my half-open window. Another middle-aged man, his face burnt to a dark brown and a white beard piercing the wrinkles on his face, grabbed the driver by the shoulder. 'You have to be a Muslim,' he said. 'All drivers are Muslims.'

But the driver kept his cool. 'Arre baba, I am a total Hindu. Murari Sharma my name is. Here look at my driving licence.' Bharat immediately butted in, 'Yes, yes, Hindu. Just like me. We are all from the press. You know, to report on what the Muslims did in Godhra.'

The man let go of the shoulder, but the snake was hungry. It had not hunted for a while and looked frustrated that this little crumb it was hoping to prey on was not Muslim. But it wanted to be doubly sure and inspected the crumb in detail. More faces started sticking to my half-open window. Face after face followed. Many of them had dark-yellow teeth with a dark blood-red outline framing them in. Others had just blood-red teeth and stank from years of chewing raw tobacco and drinking home-brewed liquor. And they kept flowing past my window, sticking their faces to the glass for a while, making their noses blunt on the glass and then moving on. After a while all the faces looked the same. As if there was just one man fragmented into a thousand faces and bodies. I had this weird sensation that if I beheaded one of them, two more heads would sprout from the stump of the throat. And if I beheaded those two heads as well, four more heads would sprout. It would be an unending process until I was buried in an ocean of heads stinking of blood, tobacco and home-brewed liquor.

The old man with the stubble-ridden wrinkles broke the chain of thought. 'Not Muslims, no?' he asked, 'Because we can always pull your pants down and check.'

The bulb of fear at the bottom of my heart burst. The lake at the base of my stomach broke through every pore of my skin in a cold sweat. Between the mob and the three men in the car, I was the only one with a circumcised penis. Had they pulled my pants down, they would have found my circumcised penis. I would not have been able to explain to them that I was a Jew, and although I had something in common with Muslims, I was definitely not a Muslim.

I was certain that no blinding light would burst out of my groin to let these people know that one man, who was the forefather of both the Jews and the Muslims, had assured

God that his children would be taught perfect devotion. That in return God had promised him that his children would survive through the generations while other peoples perished. That the pact had been inked with a little blood and foreskin from my penis and the penises of my forefathers.

But now, instead of protecting me, my penis was about to kill me. I decided to take charge. *'Arre bhai, shu bolo chho,'* I said in chaste Gujarati. *'Ahin badha Gujarati chhe. Hindu chhe. Miya koi nathi.* We are all from the press. Reporting on the Miyas that burnt the train.'

Bharat's experience came to our aid. 'Don't worry, we will not let them get away,' he said.

'Yes, yes don't let them get away! Don't let them get away,' voices shouted back.

Slowly, the pressure started to ease on the taxi. The old man with stubble-filled wrinkles moved away from the driver and the small plough was picked up from the bonnet. The constricting grip of the python loosened. The faces with red teeth pulled back. We moved forward. 'Don't let them get away,' one of them shouted. 'Jai Shree Ram,' we shouted back and slunk away.

There were no mobs after that. In some villages that we passed there were no people at all. The silence was eerie. As if the moment was about to burst into a million flames any minute. As if there was a mob hiding behind every bend.

A little ahead, Kalol town was a huge ball of fire. Shops next to the highway must have been Muslim owned. From the height of the flames, it seemed they had been burning for a while. A small group of men was busy creating a bonfire of things brought out from the shops. The rest of the crowd was made up of onlookers, lining the highway. Men stood around the flames in a relaxed manner on one leg, resting their hands on the other onlookers' shoulders. There was a strong stench of kerosene and rubber everywhere.

A small truck, loaded with hundreds of crates of eggs, was burning on the side of the road. 'One large omelette that is,' I could not help remarking.

A little ahead in a large, open field, two policemen stood bang in the centre, resting on their canes with a calm and relaxed expression on their faces. 'We have nothing to do with all this,' they seemed to say.

Another stretch of silence followed as we left Kalol and reached Halol. This town was burning too, but the roads were empty except for small groups of men standing at street corners. Someone had systematically attacked a handcart of watermelons. Not a single one was left intact. Little red pieces of the fruit's flesh lay splattered all around the burning cart. The eyes of some of the men turned suspiciously at us. We rushed on.

From then on there were only small stalls simmering. The remains of huge fires dotted the small landscape. It was only later that I realized I was extremely lucky to have survived that day. Soon, entire families would be burnt alive along with the lorries they were trying to escape in; men would be made to wear garlands of burning rubber tubes doused in kerosene. Others would be hacked or clubbed to death.

What I saw that day remained with me forever. Like grotesque postcards pinned on the walls of my mind with no way of reaching out and removing them. Sometimes I feel as if I have been tied to a chair in a room, which has nothing but white walls on which hang large photographs of dead, burnt bodies, of men lying in the middle of empty curfew-bound streets. Knives pierce their stomachs. Corpses are lined outside mass graves. Men pose with swords for photographers like victorious soldiers. Burning shops. Streaks of red blood on black tar roads. My captor has stuck my eyelids to my forehead. They water with the effort to close.

I had just finished the article on the terrorist conspiracy in Godhra when the phone rang. It was mother from Ahmedabad.

'Robin, we have to get out of Guptanagar,' she said, her voice straining with the effort of trying to remain calm.

'What?' I said a little irritated. I was used to hearing her talk about leaving the house over the smallest of crises. Once she had wanted to find a new house because three cobras had appeared in the garden in a span of two weeks. Of course it was not a small matter but it was definitely not big enough to change houses. At another time, she argued with an abusive drunk in the middle of the road, and that was good enough to find a flat somewhere and get out of Guptanagar. I was used to her panic attacks.

'We have no choice, Robin. We have to get out of Guptanagar,' she was saying.

'Mom, this is not the time to talk about shifting,' I said. 'Have you looked outside? Everything is burning. There are fires everywhere. Let all this subside and we'll think about it.'

'What do you mean "have you looked outside"? You don't understand Robin, the fires are too close. Everything is burning around the house. The fires are too close.'

This was the first time I realized that the matter was serious. That I was not a mere observer, an outsider, who encountered danger occasionally. I was an insider. 'How close?'

'I just hope the antique shop next door does not catch fire. You know how they have those huge pieces of carved wood resting on our garden wall.'

'Ask them to put the wood on the ground! They should put it on the ground!'

'Robin, it's too scary. I can see yellow flames from between the trees. There is black smoke everywhere. Everyone seems to have a sword here. They are running all over the place.'

'Lock yourself in. Lock every bloody door!'

'I have but I don't feel safe. What the hell is this place coming to! I don't feel safe inside my own house!'

'Do you have anyone with you?'

'Yes, the maids. They feel safer here. Oh hell, wait . . .' (after a pause of a couple of minutes) 'Robin, I think they just burst a tear gas shell outside. Right outside the front gate . . .'

'In front of the house? But we are away from the main road . . . Isn't all the action on the main Guptanagar road? What are they doing in front of the house?'

'They are using the dust road to run into the slum behind . . . And into the fields. Shit, Robin!'

'Oh hell!'

'Another shell! All that white smoke . . . It's choking . . . Robin, I can't talk to you right now, but we have to sit and think about it . . . We have to get out of Guptanagar . . . We can't live like this. Think of the future, Robin.'

'Mom, I am worried for you!'

'Don't worry. Tear gas means police are not far away . . .'

'Yes, you're right . . . Take care . . .'

'And don't leave Vadodara. The highways must be a bloodbath.'

'Don't worry, I am not planning to leave. Besides I won't be able to . . . I'll take care of myself and you take care of yourself.'

The next three days would be the worst in the history of Ahmedabad and the rest of Gujarat. In three days about 1500 people would die. Murdered in cold blood. Mobs much larger than the ones I had encountered had attacked entire localities and hacked its residents to death. Or started a large bonfire and flung the victims into them.

Guptanagar was like a matchstick waiting to burst into flames because of its proximity to Juhapura. A slight movement could spark a flash of madness. Even the sight of Muslims, who had no choice but to pass through Guptanagar to get to Juhapura, would lead to irate people coming out of their homes and pelting stones. Bleeding bodies would reach Juhapura and then rumours would start in Guptanagar that a mob of 5000 Muslims was gathering to attack Guptanagar and burn it down. Those mobs never came, but the rumours were enough to keep Guptanagar under curfew for a long time.

It was time for us to get out of Guptanagar and move to that part of the city where there was no curfew. Because there were parts of the city which lived on as if nothing had happened. We thought we could find a place where nothing would happen. How were we to know then that we would carry a little bit of the riot with us everywhere we went even after people had stopped talking about the bloodshed?

CHAPTER FIVE

There had been many other occasions when the David family seriously considered leaving Guptanagar and the comforts of familiarity—and sometimes even left home. But we always returned, either with our crushed dreams or failed adventures.

Like the two times that my mother, my sister and I immigrated to Israel. My mountain-climbing-near-death-experience was the third time. And because there has to be some logical explanation for what made us go through the insanity of immigrating twice, we have decided to blame my illiterate maternal great-grandmother. She had filled mother's childhood with stories from the Bible. Never having read a word of the Torah herself, she had drawn a picture of the Promised Land in her mind. How the sky would be a deep blue, the earth the colour of molten gold and the trees emerald green. She passed on this picture to mother through stories of Samson and Delilah, Moses and the splitting of the Red Sea, Noah and his ark of animals, and of course the coming of the prophet Elijah to deliver bliss on earth. At that time mother did not believe in Elijah. But she believed in the picture of the Promised Land, reinforced by postcards that relatives, who had already migrated to Israel, sent back.

So, four years after I was born, we packed and left the Guptanagar home, believing strongly that we would return only as tourists on vacation. We were housed in an absorption centre for new immigrants in the little town of Carmiel, hidden in the foothills of the Galilee. It was full of pine trees and was founded as late as 1964.

It was late afternoon on a Friday. Shabbat was about to start. We had known beforehand that in the Promised Land everything closed down from Friday sundown to Saturday sundown. One of the other new immigrants, who had been there a little longer than us, took mother to the nearest supermarket and asked her to pick up whatever food she wanted.

Mother must have been in a haze on that first day. Fighting her first jet lag on the one hand and trying to make sense of an alien system of shopping in a foreign language on the other must have been too much for her. That is the only way I can explain her coming home with a plastic bag of frozen chicken gizzards. We slept on light stomachs that night.

As if the rubbery taste of chicken gizzards was a sign of things to come, mother caught malaria after a few days. She had carried the sting of the female anopheles mosquito from Ahmedabad, and it had blossomed into a terrible trembling in Israel, where they had eradicated the disease many decades ago. Having never seen such trembling in their lifetimes before, the absorption centre authorities were certain mother had brought to the Holy Land some incurable, unpronounceable tropical disease, which would unleash an epidemic of untold proportions.

So they quarantined her in a hospital room where a nurse

brought food three times a day, and a handsome doctor who, mother told me later, looked like Gregory Peck checked her temperature at regular intervals. He visited mother's ward frequently, not because he was falling in love with her, but because he had never seen a person suffer from malarial rigours before.

She also admitted that this was perhaps the best part of her stay in Israel. She did not have to worry about finding a job or making money or sleeping with the guilt of not feeding her children enough or waking with the burden of being a failure where all immigrants had succeeded. And a handsome doctor had his finger on her pulse.

While Gregory Peck was keeping an eye on mother, my sister and I were spending time with relatives who, till then, had existed only in black-and-white photographs in my Dada's immaculately maintained photo albums. An uncle who had benignly smiled out of the photographs now demanded 'pin-drop silence' from a four-year-old boy and a six-and-a-half-year-old girl. He had the volume control knob firmly in his grasp. Make one sound above the permissible limit and he would charge out of the most unexpected corner of the house with a 'Shhhh!', stare at us to make us guilty, and then glide back into another unexpected corner.

'Our neighbours should not feel we are not cultured,' he would tell us. My sister and I would look at each other bewildered, unable to understand the relationship between silence and being cultured. His obsession with soundlessness had reached such extremes that we were not even allowed to boil an egg on Yom Kippur day. Not because uncle was religious and he firmly believed in fasting on the day of repentance, but because the neighbours would get the wrong impression if they heard water boiling on Yom Kippur and realized that the family was not fasting. In his mind, it would be proof that Indian Jews were not 'Jewish enough'.

Uncle had been badly offended when the Rabbinical had cast doubts on the 'Jewishness' of Indian Jews, when they first arrived in Israel in the early 1960s. He had taken it upon himself to prove that Indian Jews were as Jewish as anyone else from any other corner of the world. And it was starting to suffocate me.

So it was a relief to move into the house of a raucous aunt. But she packed her sea-green-tiled bathrooms with sacks of flaked rice, basmati rice and whole red chillies from India with only a small corner to shower in. I could never take my long Indian baths in that bathroom. Every morning as I took off my clothes, the stinging fragrance of red chillies coated with the scent of basmati rice would fill my nostrils. I would long to be back in Ahmedabad but did not have the courage to tell mother that, even after she came back from the hospital. But when she said she was planning to return and take on the rigours of surviving in an alien land when she was stronger physically and mentally, I jumped enthusiastically. It was better to be back in Ahmedabad than to dream of Ahmedabad in aunty's basmati bathroom.

So, within three months of landing in Israel, we caught a flight to India, to Ahmedabad, certain that the chicken gizzards had triggered a flood of troubles we could not handle. The memory of the cobbled streets of Carmiel, painted yellow with dry autumn leaves and the fragrance of pine, however, has lingered with me till today.

Six years later mother became restless again. The failure of the first attempt had given her many sleepless nights. The burden of bringing up two children, one of them handicapped, with no alimony and a degree in sculpture pushed her to try and immigrate to Israel once again. Perhaps all three of us felt a vague sense of unfinished business with Israel. We agreed to test our fortunes one more time.

We were put in another absorption centre, this time in Beersheva, a thousand-year-old city on the edge of the Negev desert where Abraham had dug seven wells to give the city its name. The balcony of our little two-room apartment, reeking of freshly polished wooden furniture, opened on to a large, dusty field where the Israeli army conducted its exercises. The sight of armoured vehicles and men in green fatigues with automatic weapons excited me. I thought I would become a soldier some day, fight enemies, become a hero. For mother however it was a constant reminder that the foundation of the Jewish nation was soaked in the blood of young men like the one I would grow up to be. But she would brush aside these thoughts and struggle hard to make Israel her home. She was determined this time and it rubbed off on us. We religiously attended Hebrew classes, tried very hard to get used to eating dry chicken and turkey not swimming in a thick broth of fragrant spices, and taught ourselves to live without chapattis. Too much bread gave me constipation but I had decided not to complain.

Surviving in Israel however needs much more than not complaining about constipation. It is an entirely different universe with its own set of laws where everything moves in reverse. If I had spent the first part of my boyhood writing from left to right, Hebrew was making me write from right to left. If India had made me open books from right to left, Israel was making me open them from left to right. If pressing a switch downward turned on electricity in India, you had to press the switch upward in Israel. Even the traffic came from the right side when I was used to seeing it rush past me from the left. And I could never get used to opening taps in the clockwise direction.

Of all these, Hebrew was the biggest hurdle for mother and me. While Amrita was already holding rudimentary conversation with Israelis on the way to the supermarket, mother and I could not tell the difference between 'Mashlomkha' and 'Ma ha Sha'a'.

'Mashlomkha is masculine for "How are you?"' Amrita would try to teach us. 'Mashlomekh is feminine. And Ma ha Sha'a is "What is the time?" It really isn't difficult, you guys,' she would insist. But language in reverse was too much for me. On more than one occasion I answered a 'How are you?' with 'Eleven a.m.' Israelis found that very funny. I did not like their sense of humour.

Then one day a navy helicopter landed on the edge of the army training ground in front of our balcony. It was a beautiful machine with patches of sea green and bright blue. Its large rotor blades kicked up such a whirring sandstorm that I could not see beyond a few metres. Only the glistening, metallic sea-green mass shone out of the dusty haze. To my boy eyes, this was a once in a lifetime event. I had never before seen a helicopter land in real life. So, while most other people rushed in and closed their doors to the sandstorm, I rushed out.

As I stood on the other side of the road separating the absorption centre from the army ground, everything started collapsing into an abstract landscape, where nothing but the flying dust and the brightly coloured machine existed. Everything else had become invisible, hidden behind the thick brown wall of dust that was hitting my face.

I remembered the strong dust-laden wind from another time, another place. A hot, burning sun, a silently sizzling afternoon, the wind, the dry riverbed. The wind lifting clouds of fine dust from the riverbed and filling an entire city with it. Ahmedabad. I was home. The helicopter was transforming into a delicate feather. A peacock feather. The dark brown bleeding into sea green bleeding into turquoise bleeding into midnight blue, floating, swimming into a wavy ocean of sand. Just like the one that had floated down with me in my dreams.

Slowly the peacock started to drift, to glide. The helicopter was lifting, taking off just as quickly as it had arrived. The dust remained suspended for a while after the helicopter disappeared, but through this opaque veil I could see the large, grey concrete block of the absorption centre, the trees, people walking around with handkerchiefs around their faces, unable to breathe like I was. The desire for Ahmedabad had been sitting in my chest like a large, black, heavy stone and it was growing bigger with every speck of dust that I breathed.

I rushed into our little apartment. 'Mother,' I said, breathless and dying to tell her that we should go back home to Ahmedabad. 'What?!' she replied in a tone sharp enough to let me know that she was in no mood to listen to me. I knew this was not the time to proclaim my love for Ahmedabad, but the desperation in her voice clearly indicated that the dust, which had filled the entire apartment, had had the same effect on her. She was thinking of Ahmedabad too. I said, 'Nothing,' and retreated into the balcony for one last whiff of the dust before it settled.

It took mother three full days to dust the entire apartment clean. But by then, the decision to return to Ahmedabad had been taken. Her problem however was that she did not know how Amrita and I felt, and she did not know how to ask us. She was riddled with guilt. Did she have the right to drag us with her while following some unfulfilled dream? The dilemma was resolved thanks to our American neighbour at the Ulpan, Amy Rosenberg.

Amy was in her mid twenties, had divorced her Christian husband and plunged headlong into religion by deciding to marry an ultra-religious orthodox Jew with all the trappings—the curly, snakelike sideburns included. She was a frail woman with thick lips and exposed no part of her body except her oblong face and thin, delicate fingers. We thought she was our friend, but she knew how to keep us at a distance. For instance, she refused to eat and drink at our table because we did not follow kosher rules. For the first time we felt as if we belonged to a lower hierarchy of people. Even high-caste Brahmins had eaten elaborate meals in our house in India. And now a member of our own people was considering our food impure.

Amy was also responsible for stamping our foreheads with the 'outsider' tag when she forgot to invite us to her wedding. The three of us were spectators from our second-storey balcony while men in black hats and black suits sang Hebrew songs and danced the Horra, their sideburns dancing with them but not keeping time with their feet. As we watched from our elevated position, the rest of the Ulpan members joined the men and fell into the rhythm of the flowing sideburns. A whirlpool of joyous humans was swirling in front of us, growing larger, thicker as more people joined in. Black hats, white shirts, black coats, brown hair, blue jeans were spinning in front of us.

Questions started dancing inside our heads. Was it because we were Indian that we were not invited? Is it possible that she did not consider us Jewish? We would definitely have been the only triplet of sunburnt faces in a wavy ocean of freckled, pink-faced Ashkenazi Jews. Would her husband have objected to suspected goys strutting around as Jews at his wedding? Or did she merely forget to invite us?

As mother told me later, that was also when she had started feeling extremely guilty for leaving Dada alone in the Guptanagar house. She could see him dozing off all by himself in the living room with a mug of rum lying untouched in front of him. She could see him crying on the shoulders of strangers, unable to bear the loneliness. And she could see her own self, sitting in the large house with a blank expression on her face, after her children had left her. The thought had made her stomach churn faster than the swirling mass of men in the wedding below. A churning that would recur periodically for the rest of her life.

The morning after Amy's wedding, mother finally popped the question to Amrita and me. 'Kids, I think I am finding it difficult here. I want to go back. What do you think?'

I don't remember what Amrita said, but I remember saying, 'Yes please . . . I don't like it here. I want to go back.' The words fell out of my mouth as if I had no control over my tongue.

'Why?' mother asked.

'The taps are too tight here,' I said.

We left Israel laughing.

CHAPTER SIX

There were other times when one of us felt some internal turmoil and strongly believed that moving to a new place would bring peace. Guptanagar was never seen as the reason for our desire to flee. It was just that we needed to flee. And because we were in Guptanagar, we had to flee from Guptanagar.

For instance, my divorced artist-writer mother, who had the capacity to conjure up distress on demand. Even after the two failed attempts at trying to make it in the Promised Land, she had considered moving to a kibbutz in Israel because of the speed at which my sister and I were growing up and becoming independent. We did not need her as much, and it had only resulted in more frequent attacks of the churning in her stomach. The thought of static isolation would crowd her heart with every inch that my sister and I grew. A kibbutz, she thought, was the best answer. The buzz of activity would drive isolation away. Luckily for her, that was just an idea that never materialized. The idea of the kibbutz was perhaps more reassuring than the actual act of moving to one.

Her children growing up was not her only fear. Like a traffic jam in the narrow lane of the Teen Darwaza area of the old city during rush hour, mother's fears would cramp up one behind the other in a haphazard, crooked line. Hardly had one fear managed to escape to some wide-open space when another came to the fore and demanded attention. In fact she has so many fears that she sometimes can't even recognize some of them. Like the fear of heights that she discovered after the riots.

The fear of snakes is one that she always had. The mere thought of a spectacled cobra, standing erect, glistening in the glow of an electric bulb at night in the garden is enough to make her run out of the house. Like that time when she had made up her mind to buy a new flat in Ahmedabad after three cobras appeared in two weeks in the garden. Cobras were not rare during the monsoons because of the fields next door, but there was always a long interval between two cobra visits. The monsoons had not yet set in at that time, which had led to more panic.

Add to this Ora's special barks designed to let us know that she was eyeball-to-eyeball with a snake standing on its tail. We had even learnt to identify the different barks. The loose but consistent bark was for the passer-by irritating her from outside the garden door. The almost playful bark was for when she was chasing squirrels. The much louder, sharp, short and tense barks were for the snakes.

It was easy to tell if there was a snake in the garden as long as Ora was there. Each time the fear-tinged barks would start, the rest of the family would freeze, abandon whatever they were doing and listen intently for a few seconds. Then a mad frenzy of activity would break out in the house, first to get Ora away from the snake and then, after Dada died, to find someone who knew how to catch snakes. In his youth Dada had spent more time hunting in the wild with the rulers of princely states than in the classrooms. He would simply put a thick napkin over his right palm, approach the snake very slowly and then suddenly grab it by its erect neck from behind. The rest of us were not designed for such acts of bravery, having spent more time in classrooms than in the wild. We could not catch snakes, poisonous, non-poisonous or man-made.

For all his bravery, Dada too was a prisoner of his loneliness. He too had, at one point, planned to leave the Guptanagar house for a mausoleum at the edge of the Dutch graves in the old city. Because of the influence he wielded in the municipal corporation as the founder of the prestigious Ahmedabad Zoo, they had agreed to give him the structure at a concession. It was a 150-year-old circular building with a dome at the top and more suited for bats to live in.

Dada was adamant about shifting. He was tired of drinking his two pegs of gin and two pegs of rum every evening all by himself. Ever since we had shifted from our rented home next to the police commissioner's office in Shahibaug to this one at Guptanagar, his drinking buddies had abandoned him. Burning fifteen minutes of petrol for two pegs of gin and the company of an old man was too much for them. Dada felt that a home in the old city would perhaps bring back his buddies, the same old days and the same old fun-filled evenings.

In the end the rest of the family convinced him that it was not worth the investment. Repairing the tomb-like structure would have eaten into half his savings, we told him, and because he was as paranoid about money as the rest of the family, he gave up the idea. Twelve years before the earthquake struck, Dada died in his own bed, wearing his usual blue-striped pyjamas and white shirt, his white hair neatly combed backwards, his thick, white moustache turned upwards to signify pride, and an expression on his face that could best be described as a smile. As if he were laughing at himself.

My sister on the other hand lived in the world of books. I am assuming she must have built a thousand homes in her mind from the thousand descriptions she must have read in a thousand books. Assuming because, during those early years, she hardly ever peeped out of the reams of paper that always surrounded her face. From the time she was in the toilet to the time she dozed off to sleep at night, she always had a book in hand, making it extremely difficult to hold conversation. The only space that she occupied in the house was the Freudian couch by the window in the living room, reading anything and everything she could lay her hands on, from Shakespeare to *The Wild Animals of the Serengeti*.

Once in a while, she would suddenly jump out of the world of books and make the most unexpected of demands. Like this one time when she said, 'Mom, I want a black-tiled bathroom. Why can't we remove all the white ones and replace them with black ones? You know, like the one Isadora Duncan had. And imagine the advantages. Robin won't be able to make it dirty even if he wanted to!'

At another time she said, 'Whoever built our house was an idiot. It should have been built right at the back of the plot. That way we would have had a large, open space in the front with a large number of trees. Like a mini forest. The way it stands right now, somewhere in the middle and more towards the front, we just have thin strips of land on all four sides in the name of a garden. Absolute insanity I tell you.'

Dada had saved a little extra money from breeding and selling Pekinese. There was a direct relationship between the fertility of the Pekinese pair and the extent to which our house grew during its initial years. Dada would add an extra room to the house each time he had a large litter. So my sister would retreat to her world of books where black-tiled bathrooms existed between clean white pages. She now lives in France with Nathaniel, their two children and a house of their choice that they built.

And then there was me. Someone more interested in running out of the house at the first given instance, as it was the best way to avoid a confrontation with Dada when he was alive. For the better part of his life, Dada had fought a grim battle with dust, spanking the entire house clean every few hours with his broom of peacock feathers. And I was always in his way.

'Get up,' he would say every couple of hours. 'How can you sit in so much dust? Let me clean it . . .'

'But you cleaned it right now,' I would counter. 'Let it be. It's okay.'

'No. Get up. I can't stand it. There is not going to be any dust in my house.'

'But what's the point? You are going to dust it right now, and before you come back from your nap, there is going to be another layer of dust all over the place.'

'Why can't you listen to me for once? Why do you always have to argue?'

'Why don't you take a nap and come back? There will be more dust to clean up then. And I will be out of here . . .'

Because these verbal battles increased by the day, I preferred to spend more time with the boys in the gully, playing cricket. By the time I came back, the sun would have set and the thin layer of dust that had settled on me would have become thick with sweat. Dada would have downed a couple of pegs of gin and his battle with dust would be over. I could loll around in the house as much as I liked and he could not have cared less.

But we were two experienced adversaries who understood each other's moves down to the last detail. It was the kind of understanding that develops only from taking on the same adversary day after day. Responses had been learnt and internalized. We did not have to think to begin or end a fight. Dada would end the night with at least another three pegs, often mixing gin with rum and whisky, wade to his bed, drawing doodles with his feet on the floor, but get up the next morning at four, fresh as the morning sun, as if he had never touched a drink in his life. And as soon as he finished bathing, oiling his white hair and combing it backwards and massaging his moustache with Brylcreem to hold it in the upturned position, his battle with dust would begin. It would also mean that I had to start looking for a reason to stay out of the house so that I did not come in the way of his crisp blows at the dust with the peacock-feather broom.

One reason dust entered our house in waves was the way in which it was built. There was not a single window in the house that we had ever closed for years together. Because if we did close them, the house and its thin walls would trap the burning forty-five degrees centigrade inside, turning it into an oven. Over the years, the hinges had rusted and if we tried to close a window the joints would crumble and fall, creating more problems. So it was better to never try and close the windows.

At the same time, we could not allow the windows to remain open because we lived close to the slums, the fields and the Vasna barrage, which fed water to the dry Sabarmati River once in a while. Together, the three were the perfect breeding ground for flies by day and mosquitoes by night. Keeping off the cloud of mosquitoes was especially important, as they were adept at raining stings on every inch of exposed flesh. After spending an entire childhood shivering uncontrollably with malaria, I had developed immunity to the mosquitoes, but it was difficult to spend night after night slapping my feet and hands. I could not even use a blanket to shield myself from the incessant bites, because if I did the still summer night, without the slightest whiff of a breeze, would become oppressive. I would start sweating in the humid night because the whirring ceiling fan would have no impact.

The only solution was to envelop the house in a wire mesh. Every single door and window had it so that the breeze could waft in, and flies and mosquitoes were kept out. Leave the wire mesh door open for a few extra seconds at night—especially after a quick downpour during the monsoon—and the mosquito cloud would forcefully push its way in as if an entry was its birthright, ensuring that your body was covered with bulbs of blood from head to toe.

The wire mesh also acted as a filter, filling the house with the beautiful dull glow of reflected sunlight. The light would bounce off the cemented red garden floor and burn parts of the house with a glow that left me with an unexplained melancholy. This was especially so during the early months of winter when the sun slanted a little more during sunset and sent a beam of yellow light from the kitchen window into the rest of the house.

But the mesh ensured that the dust entered the house without any provocation or resistance. Even a tired cyclist, going home slowly on his high, black Hero cycle after a hard day's work, could kick up a thin line of dust which would lift over the high garden wall, weave its way past the neem, eucalyptus and borsalli leaves to come and rest on the mesh for a while. Until a gusty breeze pushed it into the house and our lives. And then Dada, wielding his peacock-feather brush, would start his battle with dust all over again. And I, the one hurdle between victory and him, would have to run out of the house.

In short, all of us had thought of running out of the house at some point or another, but it was always for extremely personal reasons. A cyclone would rise inside us, threatening to blow away all that was quiet and peaceful. We could not run away from it because we could not run away from ourselves. But we had to run away from something. So we would think of running away from the house. The cyclone would however always dissipate before any one of us actually took action. And if we did leave, we always returned. It was our home, we had come to realize.

But the riots were about to change all that. This cyclone was not going to blow over in a hurry. Hindus and Muslims lived too close to each other in Guptanagar for any cyclone to dissipate, we were certain. We had to run away. Quickly. Before the fires could spread to the antique shop and leap into our house. For the first time, a cyclone of violence that had not originated inside us was making us consider leaving our home. For the first time, leaving would not remain a mere idea. We would really, truly leave. Or so we thought.

CHAPTER SEVEN

Emu eggs are among the easiest to dispose of. There is always someone who wants to adorn his living-room showcase with them and swell his chest like a pouter pigeon for having acquired such a rare object.

Over the years Dada had acquired many of these glistening, black, oblong bulbs, as big as the face of a ten-year-old child. Dada cut out small, flat holes at the two poles of these spheres so that they could stand on their own in little painted saucers. As if they had invisible spines. The balance was so perfect.

Dada would use the eggs to break uncomfortable silences with shy guests. After surveying the many objects in the living room, they would invariably point at the eggs and ask, 'What is that, Dada?'

'Buffalo eggs,' Dada would reply, poker-faced, casually sipping his gin and Limca.

'Hmmm,' the guest would say, but wrinkles of doubt would immediately start appearing on his forehead. '*Buffalo* eggs?'

'Why, aren't they as black as buffaloes?' Dada would add to the doubt with the look of an experienced zoologist on his face. But a smirk would slip out of the corner of his lips. 'Which other species can give you eggs as black as that?'

'No, you are pulling my leg . . .' the guest would say, still looking uncertain.

'Of course I am pulling your leg,' Dada would finally give out the joke. 'Only buffaloes can believe that buffaloes lay eggs!' And with that the ice would be broken. The house would be filled with laughter and the guest would lose all his awkwardness, helped with a large dose of rum or gin.

But now Dada was dead, the riots were showing no signs of ebbing, and mother and I were planning to shift to a new, much smaller flat or tenement, in which emu eggs and many other objects would not fit. There were already too many delicate things to take care of, and the last thing we needed to worry about was a set of eggs as brittle as dry flowers.

A couple of phone calls were made, and the same people whom Dada had called buffaloes were ready to take the eggs away. 'Please, please, please don't give them to anyone,' they pleaded. 'I will give you anything in return. Just wait for the curfew to be lifted and I will take them away.'

Much later we found out that they had tried to use the eggs in almost exactly the same way as Dada had—breaking ice with guests by first calling it a buffalo egg and then calling the guest a buffalo. Not always did the ploy work. There were times when guests objected to the remark and stomped out, ending friendships forever.

Mother and I, however, discovered that the more we disposed of objects like emu eggs, the more objects we unearthed from hidden corners of the house we did not even know existed. Dada could not throw anything. He simply found a new place to keep things.

At one point, we found tick powder, neatly packed in little

cardboard boxes. Dada had himself made the powder in the 1950s, a time when he did not have a job and made a living out of repairing guns and selling tick powder to the rich dog-lovers of Ahmedabad. He had not touched these boxes after 1954 and found a little corner for them in the right-hand bottom shelf of one of the three cupboards in which he kept books.

'Do you think this powder works?' Mother asked me when we discovered the boxes, thinking about Ora, who would be infested by the midget bloodsuckers once in a while. I looked at her. 'I guess not,' she said and decided to bury the powder in a hole in the garden.

In another cupboard we found a mound of wooden blocks, some as small as matchboxes, others as big as shoeboxes. 'What is that for?' I asked, exasperated as one meaningless object after another tumbled out. 'Pedestals for Dada's toys and antiques,' mother said, standing beside me with her hands on her hips.

'But he did not even have as many toys,' I said, starting to get irritable now. 'What was the man up to!'

Mother obviously knew her father better. 'You know, he had a contingency plan for everything. Even pedestals.' We decided to give these to Leelaben, our maid, who would use them as fuelwood for cooking.

As mother closed the cupboard and stepped back, she tripped over a mound of files lying on the floor. The look on her face changed. Until now it had been fluctuating between irritation and amusement. But now it was fast turning sombre. 'I have to get out,' she said and rushed out of the room which was called the library but was nothing more than an extension of Dada's bedroom. 'What happened? We still have a lot to do here,' I said, a slight headache starting to bother me.

'I can't do this now,' she said. 'I have to get out.'

'What happened? You were fine until now . . .'

She pointed at the files and said, 'You know whose letters those files contain?'

She knew that I knew that Dada never threw away a single letter. He just filed them away year-wise, subject-wise, issue-wise, person-wise. So, I said, 'I don't know, Lucifer's?'

'No. Your father's.'

This was a serious matter. When mother brought up the topic of my biological father, you stopped joking. It did not matter that I had seen him only three times in the last thirty years. His last visit was in 1977. My memory of him was that of a large man with curly hair and thick lips. And I hated it when people said I looked like him.

My first memory of father was of him exercising his visitation rights and coming to see my sister and me. I was five years old. The divorce was four years old. And he was a stranger to me. His large, six-foot frame bent down and hugged me. He tried to chat us up, but there were many awkward silences. This man was our father and we did not know what to say to him.

After a while, he felt uncomfortable, unable to hold conversation with his own children, and said, 'Okay, I think I should go now.' His face, which was twice as large as mine, had kissed me on the cheek. And yet today, his features are a blur in my mind. Like a portrait photographed in low light at one-fifteenth of a second by the shaky hands of a caffeine addict who has not had his daily fix. This picture had beady eyes, curly hair and thick lips, but it is so blurred that it represents all men with beady eyes, curly hair and thick lips.

He came to see us twice more in the next five years but that did not help improve this image. The only features that shone out of the haze were the expressionless eyes. The rest have remained out of focus.

I must accept there are times when I look into the mirror and feel the dull ghost image of an unknown man drifting along the outline of my body. I must be carrying a little bit of my father in me. The large frame and the curly hair are the same. I only hope that the eyes are not.

Mother was looking at the files as if the mound was transforming into a swarm of cockroaches. 'Dada kept his letters?' I asked. 'Why?'

'You know . . . Dada believed in peaceful co-existence . . . Experiments in love . . . All that.'

'So it was all about how to love a man your daughter hates . . .'

'Something like that. You know what I fear? That he lost his meticulous filing skills just before he died. He screwed up the entire system. So now, my letters to him during my college days are lying with his courting love letters to your grandmother . . .'

'He filed those too?'

'Yes, he made carbon copies of everything. And you know where your father's letters to him are? I think they are in one of those files in which he kept correspondence with antique dealers.'

'Oh, so he did have a convoluted logic to it all. You are the product of his love for my grandmother, and father is an antique in my mind.'

Mother was not amused. She kept looking at the files. Then she walked slowly towards the living room and sat down on the Freudian couch. Even after thirty years of the divorce, memories of a marriage filled with violence could crowd her heart with despair. To top it, Dada's inability to throw away anything. 'Why have I waited for so long to throw Dada's things away . . .' she was talking to herself. 'Why do we always wait for the past to melt by itself when we know that it doesn't?'

Mother sat silently for a few minutes as the three years of her married life rushed by in front of her. A young woman bustling with energy, armed with a bachelor's degree in sculpture and a head full of Moore, Matisse, Tutankhamen, Nefertiti and the madness of Van Gogh, marries a man who does not allow her to wear sleeveless kurtas, forces strict vegetarianism and sees ghosts in rosewood sculptures that are half-fish half-woman.

Three years later they are divorced after a bitter legal battle in which he brands her 'mentally unstable' and she decides to forfeit the alimony to convince him to sign the divorce papers.

'I have to get out of here,' she said, standing up and waving her hands to disperse the thick, black cloud of memories forming in front of her eyes. 'Have they lifted the curfew?' she asked, putting an old dupatta around her wrinkled kurta and slipping on the men's Kolhapuri chappals she has been wearing even before they came into vogue.

'Only for a couple of hours,' I said.

The Godhra attack was not even a month old. Violence was bursting out from unexpected corners of the city. Only two days ago, a thin, old man with a white beard and a skullcap was driving his autorickshaw filled with women passengers towards Juhapura when he was hit on the head by a stone not too far away from our home. The old man kept driving and then collapsed when he reached Juhapura, blood streaming down his temple and transforming his white kurta to a dark red.

He lived, but the incident was enough to send ripples of rumours in Guptanagar. Word was that Muslims were gathering at Sankalitnagar, near the entrance of Juhapura, and would attack any time. In Guptanagar everyone came out, armed with metal pipes and swords. But nothing happened. The incident was only good enough for the police to clamp a strict curfew. And now, two days later, it had been relaxed for a couple of hours for people to fill up their rations so that the streets could be closed down for another couple of days.

'Mom, I don't think it is safe to go out right now,' I said, fully aware that no one could stop her from rushing out of the house when marriage memories filled her chest. She ignored me. 'Where are you going anyway?'

'You know the Swaminarayan Avenue flats at Anjali Char Rasta? Somebody was telling me they have a couple of flats vacant there. May be cheap. I'll go look . . .'

'What's the point, mom? That's barely five minutes by rickshaw from here . . . If we have to move out, it has to be more than five minutes away . . .'

'You know better than I do that curfew begins from Anjali.' Mother had her own logic. 'That means there is no curfew there . . . I went there to buy vegetables the other day before the rickshaw-wala was attacked, and people were having fun . . . As if nothing had happened. They were eating ice creams and pizzas on the roadside, all that . . .'

Before leaving the house, mother looked into the mirror and carefully placed a large, red sticker bindi in the middle of her forehead. She loved to anoint her forehead with large, red dots, even wearing them to the synagogue at times to shock the Jews. She calls it her third eye and sincerely believes that without it she becomes weak. But now, it had a different function. She was going to a Hindu area and the bindi would be her armour, her shield. It would ensure that she would not be mistaken for a Muslim because of her white kurta and white hair. She was even starting to develop a habit of removing the bindi while passing through a Muslim area of the city, although with a heavy dose of guilt and anger.

'I'll be back,' she said. Peeping out of the door and seeing a thin line of scooters and rickshaws passing in both directions, she stepped out.

My naive understanding of the real-estate market was that normally when people want to sell homes close to riot zones they welcome anyone with open arms. If a customer turns up at their doorstep while the violence has not even quelled, they take extra care to ensure that you don't miss a single detail, like the relative coolness during summers, proximity to large supermarkets, access to the centre of the city and of course the most amicable of neighbours.

I expected mother to be gone for at least an hour, settled down on the Freudian couch to watch on television an old cricket match where Sachin Tendulkar was pitted against the mighty Australian bowling attack at Sharjah. Like most

Indian men, I had spent a large part of my boyhood dreaming about becoming a successful cricketer, a fast bowler. I had taught myself to hurl a light rubber ball at great speeds at my neighbours during roadside cricket matches, even hurting some of them with stinging bouncers. Speed fuelled my dreams. One day I shall bowl alongside Kapil Dev, be the support bowler he never had. One day I shall hurt Australian and West Indian batsmen with stinging bouncers. Like the ones that hurt our batsmen. The dream withered away quickly when I did not even make it to the school team. In the end the desire for the game had been reduced to admiring skill in the re-telecast of old cricket matches. The outcome of the match was known. You knew whether your team was going to win or lose. It allowed you to admire technique, skill, temperament. It allowed you to forget everything around you.

Besides, it was Sachin Tendulkar, your one gladiator who fought dour battles against tough opponents. I liked to watch him bat. I liked to become him. The bat was in my hands. I was hitting the ball on the rise, over the in-field, dancing down the track to fast bowlers as if they were spinners from a club team. Nothing else existed. Just the television set and me. Me and Sachin. Sachin and me. Ecstatic crowds. Screaming millions. The world was a cricket stadium. I was the hero. They were cheering for me.

But before I could nail my complete being to an old cricket match, mother was back inside half an hour. 'What happened?' I asked as she walked into the living room, her shoulders slouched, her lips pursed. 'Back so early? Did the police send you back?'

'No, the secretary of the housing society turned me back,' she said in a low voice, walked into the kitchen and came back with a glass of water, sipped it gently and said after a pause, 'They don't want people like us.'

'What is that supposed to mean?' I sat up.

'It means that he did not even show me a vacant house. They don't want people like us.' Mother's tone remained low, disturbed.

'People like us? What is wrong with us?'

'Meat-eaters. They don't want meat-eaters. Only vegetarians.' Mother was looking at the television but she was not seeing the match. She had never liked or understood the game.

'How did he know we were meat-eaters?'

Mother was still looking at the match and said, 'Well, he asked me my name. I said Esther David. So he said, "Meat-eaters, right?" I lied. I said no. But he said, "That is what all of them say. Sorry, but we don't want meat-eaters." And that was the end of that.'

Mother's gaze had shifted from the television to the floor. Something invisible and obscene was dancing in front of her eyes, and it was seen on her face.

Just then Sachin hit a towering six off someone—a powerful swing and the ball sailed into the sea of faces. The crowd erupted in singular joyous rapture. The tricolour flag was waving in a sea of bobbing black heads and blue T-shirts. Indian faces, painted with the tricolour, were smiling ear-to-ear, jumping up and down, their hands raised to the skies.

Something was sinking inside me. I was sitting in a small boat with a large hole in its bottom. An ocean was rising at my feet. Bubbles were forming at my ankles. I had never leant to swim. This ocean or any other. The joyous screams from the television were starting to hurt my ears.

Mother took the remote from my hands and switched off the television. It was a relief but only for a few sparse moments. Suddenly, everything seemed too silent. The buzz of traffic on the main Guptanagar road was thinning out quickly. The city was starting to shut itself indoors.

From a distance came the crackling sound of a police officer barking orders into an old megaphone. He was announcing that the curfew had been reimposed. 'People are hereby informed that a curfew has been imposed in the Vejalpur police station area. Strict action will be taken against those who break the law . . . Stay indoors until further orders. Do not come out of your homes or you will be severely punished . . .' The policeman was barking his orders in a sing-song manner as if he was announcing the latest act of the trapeze show. As if he were saying, 'And now ladies and gentlemen, a heart-stopping performance from our daredevil trapeze artists Raj and Neena. For the first time they will float fifty feet in the sky and change swings and that too without the safety net!' The old megaphone, barely transmitting electricity, made the policeman's voice crackle.

A cold stillness was starting to descend on us. 'Robin, I don't want your children growing up here,' mother said. 'I don't want my grandchildren to know the meaning of the word "curfew".'

I felt as if my skin was turning crisp, dry, black. My bones were melting away. I was an empty shell, as brittle, as hollow and as delicate as an emu egg.

CHAPTER EIGHT

The flapping wings of a solitary pigeon, the eternally panicky calls of sparrows and squirrels, and buzzing mosquitoes mark the beginnings of a slow-rising decibel penis in Ahmedabad every morning. The flappings and buzzings let loose independent pockets of sound into the still air that attract all other sounds around them—the grating sound of fire cutting metal at the welding workshop, the muffled thuds of men digging roads, the pastiwala belting a melodious 'Paaaaaaper' interspersed with the vegetable vendor singing 'Shaaakbhajeeeye' at fixed intervals.

They are followed by men on scooters, who seem to think their loud honking will turn into acid and melt the traffic in front of them, and the crackling drone of the three-wheeled autorickshaws and the gentle purr of sleek, new cars which are more seen than heard. And then there are more scooters, more honking and more crackling from autorickshaws and cars, until the collective hum overpowers all other sound in the city. The penis holds hands with the hum and becomes thicker, longer, larger. Its veins swell eagerly. It peaks and holds itself in position over the city. Just before the afternoon sets in to slap it with a wave of heat, the city turns into a large, deafening machine that hums uncontrollably. The flappings of pigeons, the muffled thuds and the shouting of men are insignificant satellites that revolve around this hum.

The afternoon heat silences the hum and allows other sounds to well up. Boys playing cricket in narrow gullies in the shadows of tall buildings. Their shouts of joy and despair trail behind a music band leading a marriage procession and playing a love song from a Hindi movie like a march. The march mingles with the whirr of ceiling fans and assembled air-coolers, which dissolves into the high-pitched cries of women on television soaps, which collapses into the occasional screeching of a hungry kite, swooping down from television antennas looking for sparrows to prey on.

The hum holds hands with the evening and returns to drown the whirring fans, the shouting boys, the marching band, the screaming women and the screeching kite. And then there are cars, cars, cars, scooters, scooters, scooters, autorickshaws, autorickshaws, autorickshaws, smoke, helmets, faces covered in dupattas and tired eyes scanning traffic lights to get back home.

There are of course other, more seasonal sounds, which can be heard when the hum lies shrivelled up in a corner of the city somewhere. Like when the earth turns into a hot frying pan and sizzles with the evaporating water. Or the nine nights of Navratri, when loudspeakers blare out the latest Hindi pop song set to the beat of a garba.

Even at night when the hum has shrivelled up, the city does not completely silence itself, as Frederic Aculair, a classical violinist from France who came to Ahmedabad for a performance, found out.

Frederic, a thin, pale boy with delicate features, was to perform at the open-air theatre overlooking the dry Sabarmati. He had come prepared to play his solos, his pigtails and polished shoes in place. What he did not come prepared for was the city and its constant music. It was difficult to tell if it was the high notes or the low ones that he struck, as he weaved and dodged the mosquitoes that dived around his nose and ears. Even the four mosquito repellent coils belching out strong aromatic smoke, carefully placed around him in anticipation of the attack, were not helping. But his deftly moving fingers played music all the time.

When the mosquitoes seemed to have taken a break from investigating his nasal cavities, a donkey started to bray loudly, somewhere on the dark riverbed, not bothering to keep time with Frederic's playing.

Donkeys tend to calm down quickly and this one did. But then an aeroplane took off from the Ahmedabad airport and flew directly overhead. When its loud whistle had died down, a dogfight broke out outside the theatre between rival packs of pariahs tenaciously guarding territory marked out by their urine.

But Frederic played on like a true Ahmedabadi, to whom these sounds are silence. Inaudible. We don't pay heed to these sounds which linger on like the residue of crashing cymbals.

It is only when you place a large, black hole called the curfew over the city and allow it to suck in all sound that you realize how deaf you have become to its noises. Or how deaf the city has made you. Or how deaf the city has made me. The audible penis had risen, throbbed and shrivelled up around me every day and I had totally ignored it. It did not exist. Until the curfew.

And now, the curfew had kicked this penis in the middle of the balls. It was not going to have an erection for a while. The city was lying on the floor in pain, holding itself between its legs.

On one such erectionless night towards the end of March I was lying limp on the Freudian couch watching *Xena the Warrior Princess* on television. It had been a hard day at work, going from one relief camp for Muslims to the other. I was chasing a story about missing persons. Nearly 500 families had lost one or another member of the family, and had not been able to trace them after nearly a month of the violence. They had cried, speaking about their despair at not knowing if their fathers, mothers, sons and daughters were dead or alive. When the attacks had begun, they had run blindly towards dense Muslim ghettos with whatever they could find. And only when they had the time to stand, think and shiver in fear had they realized that they had been separated from their loved ones. A month later, the uncertainty about their fate was killing them.

I had to focus hard as they narrated their sordid tales under a huge shamiana in the courtyard of the Shah-e-Alam Dargah. Behind the huge, arched-shaped gate and the tall, thick walls of the mausoleum, they were starting to feel safe. They were starting to narrate their tales more freely, and some of them sounded too fantastic to be true. As tears streamed down their eyes and touched the weather-beaten stone of this fifteenth-century structure, I realized I too felt like them. Like a refugee in my own city. How would I have reacted had I been forced to leave my home in a hurry, tie my belongings in a bed sheet and use it as a pillow to sleep on the floor of a mosque? How would I have reacted to the knowledge that my carefully decorated home was now ravaged? Dada's lifetime collection of antiques would have been looted. The rest would have been set on fire.

As the tales streamed by, I had found myself thinking how lucky I was not to be a Muslim, and had immediately felt guilty for the thought.

The guilt had competed with my concentration while writing the story. By the end of the day I was drained, and felt lucky to have a Freudian couch and a television set to openly ogle the thighs of buxom women and forget about my guilt. Ora was half resting on my stomach and cleaning her paws, Xena was letting her deadly boomerang fly and I was starting to doze off when loud screams broke out. They were out there somewhere outside my head. Must be Xena beating up a band of thugs in imaginary Greece. But Xena was not screaming. She was teasing the Greek god of war, Aries, who walked and talked like a cocky gangster from Brooklyn.

I listened, carefully this time. The shouts were coming from behind our garden wall. And then the steel thaalis began to ring. Men with steel thaalis and wooden sticks had been positioned at the edge of the fields just outside the house to warn residents if Muslims attacked Guptanagar from here. Apparently the men had seen something in the darkness. 'They are coming. Everybody out . . . Jai Shree Ram . . . Jai Shree Ram . . .' they were shouting. More voices joined in. 'I am going to kill these sister-fuckers,' I heard someone say as I stood in the garden peeping over the wall. All the men, the drunks included, were starting to swarm around the edge of the fields, dragging behind them axes, metal pipes, rusted swords and scythes. Rusted metal being dragged along the dusty road created an eerie sound. The audible penis was rising, unfurling itself from the shrivelled-up state to stand over our heads and sway with anger.

The slum-dwellers of Guptanagar were beginning to be hailed as the vanguard of the war against Muslims. Muslim shops in the area had been systematically burnt and looted in the first week of the violence itself. The handful of Muslims who had lived alongside their Hindu neighbours for years had been forced to leave and seek refuge in a camp in Juhapura. The slum-dwellers had appropriated the goats from the neighbourhood butcher Mobinbhai's shop in the initial days of the violence. They had carried the goats on their shoulders or dragged them by their ears. Mother's description of the scene was the most unexpected. 'You know those paintings of Jesus Christ standing with a lamb around his shoulders?' she had asked. 'They had carried the goats just like that . . .' It is a sight she cannot forget.

How would they have slaughtered the goats—these people who could not have known which knives to wield on the throat of the animal or how to wield them? It must have taken numerous attempts to hold the animal down so as to expose its hard neck. They must have had to wrestle with the animal in the dust. And then it must have taken a few more attempts to cut through the neck bone. The goat's body must have fluttered like the separated tail of a gecko at the first blow of an axe or a sickle. Fountains of blood must have burst out in all directions.

Did they cheer in a drunken frenzy that night as they feasted on free goat meat? I don't know. What I do know was that many residents of Guptanagar were scared ever since the first three days after the train had been burnt at Godhra. They were expecting revenge attacks all the time. They had even worked out elaborate and outlandish scenarios for a possible Muslims attack on Guptanagar. There was one in which the Muslims would first instigate a skirmish on the Guptanagar main road, pelting stones on Hindu homes and perhaps even firing a few rounds from their home-made pistols. As the Hindus of Guptanagar got ready to repulse the attack, a horde of Muslims would charge down from the fields behind, armed with heavy explosives and AK-47s and destroy Guptanagar. So guards had been posted at the edge of the fields.

Mother rushed down from the bedroom. 'What is happening?' she asked, standing at the landing on the staircase. Since the first three days after the violence erupted this was the first time that she had heard shouts so close to the house.

For a moment I was lost. Hadn't all this had happened before? The wall of sound building up outside, the startled look on mother's face, the rushing down the staircase . . .

The earthquake.

Then, I had rushed down the staircase. Mother had been standing at the bottom of the stairs with a perplexed look on her face. The wall of unintelligible sounds had been building up outside immediately after the earthquake had struck. One year later, I had taken my mother's place. And mother, mine.

Mother ran down the stairs and shook me. 'Robin, quick!' she said in a state of panic. 'Switch off all lights!' We rushed into the drawing room. 'And don't forget to put a leash on Ora . . .'

'What?' I asked.

'Just do what I say. Put a leash on Ora!' She was almost pleading. 'Just in case we have to run out, I don't want to leave her behind.' Too many things were recurring but we had no time to dwell on them when a horde of bloodthirsty Muslims was about to attack us.

I lunged towards the leash, hanging behind the door in the kitchen, and mother ran towards the switchboard. She first switched off the lights in the garden that we normally keep on for the whole night, and then she switched off all the lights in the house.

We sat down in the living room in total darkness, me holding on to a leashed Ora and mother holding on to something I couldn't see clearly. I could tell in the darkness that Ora was staring at me with her large, black eyes, unable to understand why mother and I should choose to sit without saying anything to each other at that hour. Never in our lives had we sat like this—motionless in the dark. When there were power cuts, we knew how to find our way to the kitchen where we kept the torch, the candles and matchbox without bumping into the furniture.

Minutes passed by but nothing happened. The voices outside started to rise and fall, signifying confusion. The crowd seemed to be breaking up with people going back to their homes when someone said, 'Look! There! Something moved just behind that hut!' and the leaving people rejoined the swarm, shouting, cursing, letting their rusted tools scratch thin furrows into the sand.

A palpable bubble of tension was forming around us and becoming larger and thinner with every passing moment. The people and the horde were pushing hard at the walls of the bubble but it refused to burst, only growing larger and thinner. Mother and I were cringing, waiting for that ear-shattering final blast of the bloody battle between the men in the fields and the slum-dwellers of Guptanagar. But it was taking too long. The bubble would not burst. And we could not cringe forever.

Sitting in forced darkness, however, can give you some illuminating common sense. I realized that the darkness was unlikely to transform into a protective shield around us. It was unlikely that the horde would ignore our house because it was not lit. More likely it would be targeted *because* it looked empty. 'If there is something or someone in the fields, we should be able to see it from the roof,' I told mother.

'No wait, let's call the police . . .' she said with fear.

'Let's go up and see. If there is anything, we will call the police from my cell phone,' I said, putting my hand around her to calm her.

'I am scared, Robin,' she said in a thin, wobbly voice. I was scared too. If an attack were to take place, we would be the first to suffer. There was only a single file of huts between the fields and us, and it would be easily run over. We had nothing to defend ourselves with except two ancient hunting knives from Dada's collection of antiques, a pair of garden scissors, a sickle and a couple of Swiss army knives. The one air rifle that we had once owned was stolen the day Dada died, while the rest of the family was engrossed in the final rites. Not that an air rifle would have provided any protection, but at least its presence in the house would have given us a sense of security.

Besides, we could not even run away, caught between a possible bloody battle and the curfew-bound street where agitated policemen patrolled. How would I gather all my things? How would I carry them and run with mother on one side and Ora on the other? At that moment I knew exactly what those living in the refugee camps must have felt. It was helplessness. As if a horde of killers had already surrounded us and was mocking us with, 'We are going to kill you and there isn't a thing you can do about it.' Yes I was scared. But I could not tell mother of these fears. If I did she would panic further and that would have helped no one.

So I said, 'It doesn't look like anything.' She transferred what looked like a bag from her right hand to her left and we went to the roof.

'Can you see anything? Is there anything?' mother asked, peering into the night from the roof. From where we stood, there were hutments to the east and west of the house. In front of us were the dark fields with the odd light burning like sprinkled confetti. There was nothing else. No formless shapes running towards us, no burning torches, no signs of panic. The screaming and shouting were taking place only at the edge of the fields just outside our house.

'Go, rush, rush, get me my sword, hurry up,' a man was telling someone, probably his younger brother.

'You whore, what are you doing outside?' a drunk was screaming at his wife. 'Go home now!'

But the wife was more interested in taking her husband back with her. 'What, are you going to fight in this state? Come along!' she said and dragged him by his wrist. The man followed, wobbling and grumbling, drawing doodles in the sand with his bare feet.

'Look, there,' another man was pointing at darkness in the south-east direction. 'Can you see movement there?' he said. 'I am telling you something moved there.'

Other men peered harder. 'Arre, just follow my finger. There!' They soon started seeing shapes; there were hums and haws of affirmation, followed by screams and curses. Some men started banging their swords and axes into the ground shouting, 'Come you mother-fuckers, come! I'll show you!'

While a few were almost certain that they could see hundreds of men running towards them in the darkness, others looked on suspiciously. They had not made up their minds yet on whether to see a horde or not. The steel thaalis were ringing all the time. I tried to look in the direction that the men were pointing. If so many men could see the horde, it had to be there.

'Is something there, Robin?' mother asked again.

'Not that I can see . . .' I said.

Mother brought out a powerful flashlight. 'Use this,' she said.

I took the flashlight and pointed the light into the black fields, illuminating large patches with the dull yellow glow. Wild shrubs gave out large, ominous shadows under the light.

The earth was coarse and bumpy, making the light dance and glide.

Suddenly the men broke into an even wilder frenzy. 'Jai Shree Ram . . . Jai Shree Ram,' they were shouting, hitting their swords and axes even more fiercely into the ground. My flashlight was the culprit. They must have thought it was the Muslims who were aiming the light at them. Or that the Muslims were running towards them with burning torches in their hand to make the light dance like that.

'Mom, I think I must tell them it was me . . .' I said and decided to go down to speak to the men. 'It is obvious there is nothing there.'

'No, no, no! You are not going anywhere!' mother panicked. 'How do you know there is nothing there?'

Luckily for mother and me, the men who had so far remained indoors now came out to censure the mob. 'Go home you fools,' one of them said. 'There are enough and more policemen around. We don't need an army of our own. If something happens, they will take care of us.'

Some men started moving homewards, looking suspiciously behind their shoulders, but others were still uncertain and kept peering into the fields. They too were soon convinced to leave and let everyone sleep in peace. The audible penis seemed to be shrivelling up and collapsing invisibly into the city. The silence returned.

Only when we came down to the living room and switched on the lights did I look at what mother was holding on to. 'What is that?' I asked.

'My runaway bag . . .' she said, clinging on to it even tighter, as if it were a little baby. I knew that it would have everything from our passports to an extra pair of underwear and socks for both of us. Mother had perfected the art of packing runaway bags during the earthquake. Had it not been for the earthquake I would not have believed that the essentials of her fifty-five years and my thirty-one years could be packed into one large, green rucksack. And I suspect that to be one reason she relaxed so easily once the men had left. She went back to sleep within minutes. She knew that if she had to run out she would not be without the bare necessities.

As I lay down in my bed I started wondering what it is that makes men point fingers into the darkness and see hordes where nothing exists. Do they see a collective ghost at such moments? Is it a common formlessness in all their minds? Or do they create multiple ghosts, each imagining his own version of the horde?

There is only one other story where the silence of Ahmedabad has given birth to ghosts—Rabindranath Tagore's 'Hungry Stones', the story of a cess collector in the service of the Nizam of Hyderabad who falls madly in love with ghosts.

Tagore wrote of Ahmedabad's Mughal palaces en route to England, 'The fountains play no longer; the songs have ceased; no longer do snow-white feet step gracefully on the snowy marble. It is but the vast and solitary quarters of cess-collectors like us, men oppressed with solitude and deprived of the society of women.' 'Hungry Stones' is located in quiet Shahibaug, once part of the palace of the Mughal royalty, until the Britishers used it as a residence for their officials. The state government has turned it into a badly maintained memorial to the Iron Man of India, Sardar Vallabhbhai Patel.

Not everyone has access to the room in which Tagore wrote that famous short story. Situated on the first floor, it is kept locked most of the time and you have to ask the caretaker to unlock the entrance. A flight of uneven stairs takes you to the room, containing nothing but a bust of the great poet, which looks more like black rock that has melted on a wooden pedestal. The yellowish plaster on the wall, which is peeling off, does not go well with the freshly whitewashed ceiling. There is also a life-size portrait of the poet, which seems to have been enlarged from a badly designed textbook. And yet it is not difficult to imagine a poet-author sitting alone and conjuring spirits. As you look out of the little balcony with its knee-high parapet, you can sense some of Tagore's ghostly inspiration. Between you and the cooling towers of the Ahmedabad Electricity Company at a distance is a sea of sand with a thin trickle of water that Tagore speaks of. The dry riverbed has more of the acacia than water. The only other sight is a rusty railway bridge.

As you go closer to the pedestal you realize that a few lines by the poet on Ahmedabad are embossed on it in gold print. The thick film of dust makes for difficult reading. Elsewhere he writes about this time:

> I would stay out, and work hard as long as possible, then return home at night jaded and tired, go to bed and fall asleep. Before a week had passed, the place began to exert a weird fascination upon me. It is difficult to describe or to induce people to believe; but I felt as if

the whole house was like a living organism slowly and imperceptibly digesting me by the action of some stupefying gastric juice.

Perhaps the process had begun as soon as I set my foot in the house, but I distinctly remember the day on which I first was conscious of it. It was the beginning of summer, and the market being dull I had no work to do. A little before sunset I was sitting in an arm-chair near the water's edge below the steps. The Susta had shrunk and sunk low; a broad patch of sand on the other side glowed with the hues of evening; on this side the pebbles at the bottom of the clear shallow waters were glistening. There was not a breath of wind anywhere, and the still air was laden with an oppressive scent from the spicy shrubs growing on the hills close by.

As the sun sank behind the hill-tops a long dark curtain fell upon the stage of day, and the intervening hills cut short the time in which light and shade mingle at sunset. I thought of going out for a ride, and was about to get up when I heard a footfall on the steps behind. I looked back, but there was no one.

As I sat down again, thinking it to be an illusion, I heard many footfalls, as if a large number of persons were rushing down the steps.

He went on to see much more as the story unfolds, like the ripplings in the Susta created by an invisible nymph's invisible curled hair, the simultaneous murmur, as if the nymphs were awakening from a black dream of 250 years. Like mystic forms they brush past him with their quick, bodiless steps, loud, voiceless laughter and a fragrance dispersed by a single breath of the spring. The Arab women in orange pyjamas try to entice him and the Negro eunuchs sleep with naked swords between their legs.

After that night on the rooftop, I have often wondered if the men at the edge of the fields had felt quick, bodiless steps and heard loud, voiceless voices too. There had to be something that bound together Tagore's inspiration and the men who flung abuses at the darkness that evening. After all, the great poet was inspired to write his ghost story in a very silent part of Ahmedabad and nowhere else.

What I did not expect was that other people's demons would enter my head. But they did.

CHAPTER NINE

Riots can strain the strongest of friendships. Differences that did not matter earlier become significant now. You develop a riot filter. You silently judge people in your head. 'Does this man rub his hands with glee when a death is reported, or does he hang his head in shame?' you ask yourself again and again, and accordingly decide whether he is worth your time, your attention. Conversation invariably drifts towards the subject of the riots without having to make any effort, and within minutes you know exactly where the other person stands.

But then, just when you feel you have devised a foolproof method to sieve out riot believers from riot non-believers, other questions crop up. 'I like the man but I hate his opinions, his world view. Is it possible to separate the man from his opinions? Aren't the man and his opinions one and the same? If it is possible to separate the two, what is more important, the man or his opinions? If it is not possible to separate the two, would it be fair to totally reject the friendship because I dislike his opinions, his world view?'

Such thoughts became unbearable when it came to friends like Jayendrasinh Sisodiya, a professor of English at a local college. I had met him casually at a roadside tea stall in 1995.

He had trampled all over my inhibitions of starting conversations with unknown people by approaching me and talking about books and movies as if he had known me for years. He could start a conversation with anybody anywhere. It amazed me.

On just our second meeting he had told me about his job and its frustrations. 'Can you imagine teaching English literature to insolent, malicious boys . . .' he had said. 'And it has to be something as insipid as English literature. You can't talk to them about the magic of the South Americans and the ability of the Russians to create a continuous sense of impending disaster. It has to be bloody Chaucer.'

Jayendrasinh also had his own logic. For instance, he would question the basis of an article on a couple of starvation deaths in north Gujarat. 'There has to be a pattern of death over a large area to justify a story on starvation deaths,' he would say. 'You can't go running after two dead people and scream about starvation deaths.' We would spend hours together, in the process building a bond that we thought was unshakeable.

Inevitably, during such conversations, his hatred for Muslims would erupt from the depths of his being. 'You seculars don't realize,' he would say, 'you are up against a race that is out to screw the world. By the time you realize it, it will be too late.' The term 'pseudosecular' had not entered his vocabulary till then. But Jayendrasinh knew how to cap his occasional outbursts of his dormant volcanic anger, and we had continued with our friendship.

Ever since 28 February 2002, however, I wanted to choke Jayendrasinh each time he disagreed with me. The volcano had come alive and I was not sure if running away was the right thing to do. He strongly believed that it was only natural for Hindus to hit back and 'teach the Muslims a lesson'. It was a very clear black-and-white, us-and-them world for him. So he would say, 'It was not we who started it. It was they. How can we be blamed for the bloodshed? Why are you ignoring the fact that it is they who burnt the train?'

'Who is "they"?' I would ask him. 'Every single Muslim in the world? Did every single Muslim converge on Godhra to burn the train?' I would argue that it was not fair to make broad generalizations and look at all Muslims through the viewfinder of hate, that all Muslims were not bloodthirsty just because one mob of Muslims had become bloodthirsty.

'But then why haven't they openly criticized the train burning? Why did they not condemn it?' he would ask.

'Does that prove that they are all traitors?' I would ask and he would immediately brand me as a pseudosecular. With the riots, he had made the transition from 'secular' to 'pseudosecular'. He would draw me into his mire of with-us-or-against-us arguments, and I did not know which side to take. I was being told that if I did not support the Hindus 'in this battle' I was anti-Hindu. If I was anti-Hindu, I was pro-Muslim. If I was pro-Muslim, I was an anti-national, and in effect a terrorist and a spy of Pakistan. Because all Muslims are terrorists and spies of Pakistan. And all those who support them are collaborators. That included us pseudosecular.

'But I am not supporting anyone,' I would say. 'I am not supporting you and I am not supporting the Muslims who walk the streets with swords in their hands.' But a large, black hole would suddenly open up between us and the words would be sucked in before they could reach him.

Often I had wondered why I suffered Jayendrasinh's tirade. Why did I sit with him at roadside stalls when he had made it a habit to bring up the topic of the riots with unnerving regularity and call me a traitor? Why did I not end this friendship? I could get up and leave and never turn back. There had been so many instances when I told myself that I would never again talk to this man. And yet I gravitated towards his sharp-edged arguments and blunt opinions again and again in the hope of finding something more eternal than riots between us. He had the capacity to give me a glimpse of abstract eternity drifting between us, but then he would just as quickly shroud it with riot talk.

Again I was sitting down with him at a roadside stall, sipping over-boiled tea from a broken cup and thinking about all the times I had told myself I would never meet him again.

Barely two weeks had passed since the bearded old man had been stoned in Guptanagar. The police had not yet lifted the curfew as violent battles erupted almost every night on the Ring Road, which divided Hindu Guptanagar from Muslim Juhapura. The violence hadn't claimed anyone yet, but shops were set on fire and crude bombs exploded. Men gathered at the edge of Guptanagar guaranteeing that one final push would bring the end of Juhapura once and for all. But they just kept standing there, never daring to charge in. Then the police would arrive and within the hour everything would calm down.

Though it had been almost a month of hearing crude bombs and tear-gas shells every night, I was finding it difficult to get used to them. Much as I was finding it difficult to digest Jayendrasinh's tirade. But there was no way I could have prepared myself for what he said that day.

'They deserve it, those bandias,' he said, slouching over a rickety stool and blowing into his cup.

It was only minutes before night would replace dusk. The sky had turned a deep pink. I could not see Jayendrasinh's face clearly when the tea shop owner lit a match and put it to the wick of his kerosene lantern. A warm, yellow glow lit up one half of Jayendrasinh's face, highlighting his high cheekbones, thin lips and large eyes.

'Uh?' I asked. I knew what bandias meant, but I could not believe he was saying it to me.

'You know . . . the chopped dicks,' he said. 'Those circumcised bastards. You know what bandia means, right?' He could say such things without gesticulating too much. He would just sit there, holding the cup between his palms and delicate fingers.

'Well . . . let me enlighten you my friend, I am circumcised too.' I thought I could stem the outburst by pinning the insult on myself. The steam from the tea was washing on to my specs, making them opaque and the world around me temporarily fuzzy and diffused. I liked that.

'Yes, but you are Jewish. You are different,' he said dismissively.

'Yes, but my circumcision is no different. Just in case you still haven't understood, you insult a circumcised dick anywhere in the world, you insult me. Have you seen a circumcised penis?'

'Now don't start flinging pseudosecular bullshit at me,' he said, still blowing into his cup.

'I am not flinging anything at you. I am letting you know that, technically, I am a bandia too. Whether you like it or not.'

'Come on . . . You know I wasn't talking about you . . .'

'What do you think a mob is going to find if it caught me and pulled my pants down? A circumcised dick. As circumcised as any other. Do you think I can pull up my pants and casually walk away from them as if nothing had happened? I'll most probably end up with two circumcisions, one in my dick and the other in my throat . . . Maybe that is why I don't hate Muslims so much. We share the Brotherhood of the Circumcision.'

'You are a Jew! How can you talk like this? You should hate them too. Just look at what they have done to Israel . . .'

'Please . . . I don't think of the Intefada every time I see a white skullcap and a beard in Ahmedabad. And I don't feel angry when I see them pelting stones at the Israeli army. Don't blame me for not fitting into your stereotype of the Jews of the world.'

'You are just doing drama . . . You're one odd fucker. Jews around the world hate Muslims but you have to stand out and wave the white flag . . .'

'I think I can talk like this because I am a Jew, but let's not get into that. What I can't understand is why you hate them so much . . .'

'Isn't it obvious? They are out to screw the world. Take any conflict in the world. Any conflict. And they have a hand in it. Take the Middle East, take Yugoslavia, take Afghanistan, take Kashmir . . . Take any of the riots before this one and you will see that more Hindus have died than Muslims. And who started this riot? It was they. For me that is solid proof.

They can't live in peace. Where were you pseudoseculars when the Pandits were made to flee their home and sleep on the pavements in Delhi's biting cold? You have this great ability not to see things lying right in front of your nose.'

'So according to you, the Muslims of Gujarat must be punished for what happened to the Pandits of Kashmir. The Muslims of Ahmedabad deserve brutal deaths for the Intefada in Israel and the war in Yugoslavia?'

'You have to see the larger picture, put things in perspective. They are being trained in their schools to spread their poison across the world. Besides, look at the way they are producing children with their four wives . . . I am telling you they will overrun us. Didn't you hear of the number of cases of Muslim men entrapping Hindu women and converting them to Islam? It's frightening . . .'

'So according to you, every Muslim boy of Gujarat can be motivated into seducing Hindu girls as part of a conspiracy to overrun the country.'

'Yes.'

'Don't you want to credit the girls with a little more intelligence? I think they are smarter than you make them out to be. I would like to think that they will not fall for conspiracies as easily as you have.'

'Robin, look at the larger picture . . .'

'Okay, what would you say if I fell in love with a Hindu girl tomorrow and wanted to marry her? Would that be seen as a conspiracy?'

'Robin, I have said this before and I will say it again. You are different. You are a bandia, yes, but you are a different kind of bandia.'

'Stop this bandia bullshit or you are going to get it from me . . .'

'Why you have to keep losing your cool like this I don't understand. You are different and that's it.'

'Anyway, what I still can't understand is how you can justify killing so many people just because one mob killed sixty people from your community. You are telling me that if I kill you, a mob will be justified in lynching all the Jews of Ahmedabad.'

'Yes, it is called collective punishment. Everyone has to suffer for the acts of a few. Only then will they learn a lesson.'

'Are you sure you haven't suddenly gone deaf? Can you hear yourself speak?'

'Crystal clear.'

'Boy . . . people like you would happily relive the Holocaust. You would build gas chambers all over again. Why don't you do the world a favour . . .? Put a gun to your mouth and shoot yourself . . .'

'Stop it! I don't know why you have to keep doing this, losing your temper like this. Why can't we have our differences and still be friends?'

'Fuck our friendship—where the fuck is your reasoning? A government is behaving like the mob, and you see nothing wrong?'

'Look, you can't look at everything rationally. This is an emotional issue. It has to be looked at from the heart. There was so much pent-up in the Hindus, years of oppression, it had to—'

'What oppression? Which oppression? Where oppression?'

'You will not understand . . . You will not understand.'

'And thank god for small mercies.'

Jayendrasinh could see my temper rising. Slowly, he changed the topic. He veered the conversation towards his growing attraction for yoga. How ten minutes of meditation every day had made him realize that for the last so many years he had not spent a moment with himself. He was talking about the importance of the self, when he realized I was not listening. My eyes were shifting from his face to the traffic on the road to the pink sky behind him that was slowly taking on the night hue. My ears were already on the curfew-bound Guptanagar road engulfed in complete silence.

He stopped his monologue. For the first time there was an awkward moment of silence between us. I got up and left, still seething. I put my hands in my pockets to stop myself from going for his neck and shaking him. We had been playing the game of logic so far but he had started playing a new game within the old game, the rules of which I did not know. I felt as if he had rushed ahead of me and was mocking me from a distance as I slipped and fell, unable to play two games with different rules at the same time.

I had to learn this new game.

CHAPTER TEN

'Collective punishment' was ringing in my ears as the autorickshaw dropped me at Anjali Char Rasta, the point from where curfew began.

And with it began the zone of silence. The streetlights winding down the road were a delicate, sparkling garland suspended in mid-air. This snaking curve illuminating the two kilometres towards my home only helped to accentuate the emptiness. The road, as black as the night, was divided by a two-feet-high block of concrete snaking parallel to the streetlights, and was framed on both sides by layers of creamy dust. I stood in the middle of Anjali Char Rasta, facing northwest. To my right, life hummed with the thousand sounds of autorickshaws, scooters and laughter. Headlights of cars drew temporary doodles on my spectacles as they bobbed up and down on speed breakers. Human voices sped past my right ear as people rushed in and out of areas that were not curfew bound.

My left ear was submerged in total silence except for the distant sound of an invisible policeman guarding his beat somewhere behind the Hajam Mojam, tapping his lathi on the road at regular intervals. Metal poles had been laid across the road to stop people from driving past. A group of four policemen sat at the edge of the zone of silence talking quietly.

I had walked this road a few times in the initial days of the curfew and knew what to expect. After the initial row of nondescript flats came the Hajam Mojam ki Dargah, a 400-year-old mausoleum, which had turned black with age. It was a huge cube into which arched doors and a gallery had been carved out. It had a large, sensuous, taut, breast-like dome and minarets on its four corners. Someone had tried to blow up this structure with a crude bomb in 1992 in the aftermath of the Babri Masjid demolition, but its five-feet-thick walls were not even scratched by the loud, echoing explosion. Now of course there would be nothing there but the dull-blue glow of a kerosene stove emanating from inside as the policeman on duty prepared a sparse meal, while another stood guard with his rifle.

The walk up to the Hajam Mojam was the most difficult. I had always walked this stretch as quickly as I could, because the hum of autorickshaws and scooters mingling with the occasional laughter of girls trailed behind me like an irritating stray bitch wagging her tail in the hope of a crumb. And because sound is not a stray bitch, I could not even shoo it away. The only option was to walk as quickly as possible past the Hajam Mojam where the silence was complete.

Ahead of the Hajam Mojam was the main market of Vasna area with a shopping complex and the Ahmedabad Municipal Transport System bus terminus to the right side. Had it not been the curfew hour, the place would have been abuzz with traditional grocery shops, one man nestled between sacks of grain and glass cabinets full of colourful tetrapacks. Now of course there would be nothing there but a long line of steel shutters and large locks.

Ahead of the market, to the left was the Vasna telephone exchange, a large block of concrete with a trimmed garden in the front and high walls. Next to it was the GB Shah Science College. I had never entered it but its large, unpainted grey walls and closed windows brought to my mind the image of dingy rooms with urine marks that stank.

From here the landscape suddenly changed. The skyline became short and stubby. To the right, behind a thorny veil of acacia, was the Vasna police chowki, a collage of asbestos sheets and bricks with a patch of a lawn and two wild flower plants growing on one side and two tall Kutchi horses tied behind a heap of hay on the other side.

About fifty metres from here began Pravin Nagar, and a long line of makeshift sheds that sold large wooden doors and windows, removed from havelis in the old city, which were themselves pulled down to make way for shopping complexes. The sheds were made up of asbestos sheets standing on stilts, packed with long queues of wooden frames with doors and windows, and went right down the road to Guptanagar about 200 metres away and from there to Juhapura. Behind the sheds on the western side was a sprawling cobweb of hutments, the slum of Guptanagar.

Once in a while, a shed-owner would place one of his larger doors with intricate carving outside the shed by the roadside to attract prospective customers. The sight would always amuse me. There were no insides to this door to hide, or protect or preserve, and there were no outsides to go to. People, cows and dogs walked all around it. Children sometimes used it as stumps for their roadside cricket matches.

But since the curfew, there was nothing but the road, the dust and the streetlights. The doors had been dragged in behind the rickety wooden gates from where suspicious eyes peered out.

About 300 metres from Pravin Nagar was Guptanagar and the Prabhat Driving School with its adjoining dust road on the left side. My home was about fifty metres down the road. If you walked on straight without turning towards my home, you would reach the city's municipal limits, and the large, circular building of the Agriculture Produce Market Committee (APMC), the hub of the biggest potato and onion sellers in the city.

The road turning right from the APMC was the Ring Road that led to the Satellite area where Jayendrasinh lived. On the eastern side of the Ring Road, behind the APMC, lived the Muslims in their shanties. On the west lived the Hindus in their shanties. People often refer to this road as the border between Ahmedabad's India and Ahmedabad's mini-Pakistan. Here is where the street battles took place. Here is where the gunshots were heard. Here is where Hindu and Muslim shops looked like rotting carcasses after they had been burnt down.

Past the city municipal limits you would reach a junction of three roads. One went straight to Juhapura. The one veering left was National Highway Number Eight going to Mumbai, more than 500 kilometres down the road.

'Hai bhai, do you want to go somewhere or are you going to spend the rest of the night in the middle of the road like this?' the autorickshaw driver asked sarcastically as he looked at me standing in the middle of Anjali crossroads. 'If you want to just stand then pay me and let me go . . .'

'No, no, I have to go, but to Guptanagar . . .' I said, my body starting to ache with exhaustion. 'Can you take me to—'

'No, no, no, no . . . I am not coming to the Border,' he said panic-stricken. 'Just pay me and let me go . . .'

'Wait, I'll pay you extra,' I said quietly, trying to show as much patience as I could. 'Turn right from here. We'll take one of the inside roads which will bring me at least up to the Vasna police chowki.'

'Na bhai na . . . I am not going to get killed for a little extra cash,' he said, now starting to get restless, but I knew he was lying. Every last penny mattered to people like him who most probably scratched a living by renting someone else's autorickshaw for eight hours. At the end of the day he would have to pay his rent no matter how much he had earned in those eight hours. Besides, a curfew had been clamped down on most of the old city on the eastern side, and many people had their own vehicles on the western side, making it increasingly difficult to feed large families. I knew that if I goaded him a little, he would take me anywhere I wished.

'Arre yaar, don't worry. It's all open on the inside roads,' I said, assuming that he was afraid of the curfew policeman. I wasn't lying either. On this stretch, curfew had been imposed only on the main Guptanagar road. The by-lanes buzzed, even if a little thinly, with normalcy.

My shoulders were starting to sag. The ticklish feeling of tiredness was starting to climb up from my aching calves. 'Anyway, what does the meter say?' I finally asked.

He lit a matchstick, held it close to the meter with the broken speedometer and allowed the glow to light up his bony face, his buck-teeth and thin moustache. 'Thirty-five rupees,' he said.

'I'll give you twenty rupees extra above the meter if you take me behind the police chowki,' I said, my voice almost pleading.

He stepped out of the autorickshaw, stood with his hand on his waist and looked east in the direction that I wanted him to go taking one of the by-lanes west of the police chowki. Twenty extra rupees is a lot of money for an autorickshaw driver in times of curfew.

'There are no Mohammedans here, no?' he finally asked. 'Because you educated kinds may not know, but these Miyas can't be trusted . . .'

'You know the Miyas live in Juhapura and that is far from here,' I said and sat in the passenger seat of the autorickshaw. 'Come on . . . Let's move.'

'No, no, it is better to be sure than to get into some lafda . . .' He sat in the driver's seat, yanked the lever to start the engine, and then said, 'I can't afford to die, uh . . . I have a big family to feed. If I see any trouble, I will turn back and leave . . .'

'You think I can afford to die?' I retorted. 'You are not the only one with a family. These are all Hindu homes, so don't worry . . .'

The autorickshaw started moving. I wished the driver would shut up and drive quietly, but he was in the mood to talk. 'Arre bhai, don't lose your temper with me,' he said changing his tone and becoming almost friendly. 'These are bad times. Who knows what people will do . . . And these Miyas, I tell you, all of them have guns. Our boys fight on the streets with swords like real soldiers. And they will just shoot from behind walls like eunuchs. So many Hindus they have killed.'

I did not respond, hoping he would get the message that I had had enough of Miya-bashing. I just wanted him to drive quietly through quiet lanes that would emerge behind the telephone exchange and the police chowki. I had always envied the appearance of normalcy on these lanes despite being so close to the curfew-bound areas. Technically, they were under curfew as well, but there wasn't the slightest hint of the oppressive silence that we had to bear with in Guptanagar. We drove past old couples taking languid walks after dinner, teenagers standing around in small groups in the glow of streetlights, some scratching their balls, others picking at their teeth as they whiled away their time. Some shops were still open and doing brisk business. The ice-cream parlour with the sloping tiled roof seemed especially busy as people stood around licking at cones.

The driver relaxed. 'You know these Miyas . . .' he told me, 'they have started hoisting the Pakistani flag on their windows, especially in Juhapura.' His voice took on the tone of someone who was revealing a conspiracy that only he knew of.

'Really?' I asked. 'You saw it with your own eyes?'

'Arre, I am telling you they are hanging Pakistani flags,' he said.

Normally, I would ignore such comments, not wanting to get into a verbal duel. But my anger against Jayendrasinh was still simmering and it was deflected on to the rickshaw-wala. 'But did you see it with your own eyes?' I asked again.

'No, but I know they are doing it,' he sounded uncomfortable with the probing.

'How do you know?' I asked. 'Have you been to Juhapura lately?'

'What are you saying?' he mocked me. 'I may be illiterate but I am not stupid . . . You would be chopped to pieces and fed to stray dogs if you went to Juhapura right now.'

'So then how do you know they are hoisting Pakistani flags? You are just repeating something that someone told you and I am almost certain that he too must have heard it from someone else.'

'Arre bhai, I was just . . .' he tried to defend himself.

'You were just trying to spread a rumour. That's all.'

There was perfect silence after that, broken only when we reached the back of the police chowki, and I asked, 'How much?'

'Sixty-five rupees with the extra twenty,' he said. I could tell from the way he was looking at me that he wanted to ask me something and was hesitating, but then he put it bluntly without any cushioning prologue, 'Are you Mohammedan?'

'Why do you ask?' I asked.

'No, no, just like that.' He looked embarrassed.

I wanted to say, 'Yes,' pull down my zipper, show him my penis with the missing foreskin and ask him, 'What do you want to do about it?' Instead I told him, 'Brother, if I was a Muslim in these parts, I would be chopped to pieces and fed to stray dogs.' He turned around quickly and left.

I had made it a habit to walk home from the back road on the south-eastern side of the house so that I could avoid the main Guptanagar road. Back roads were never under curfew even during the worst days of the riots.

This particular back road was parallel to the main road leading straight home. It allowed me to avoid weary policemen who did not know me. I had to pass through a snaking slum along the edge of the fields to reach home. Normally I kept my eyes and ears wide open while passing through the hutment. I had to beware of a number of things, including stray cattle and human faeces. But most of all it was important to make eye contact with at least a handful of the slum-dwellers that I had grown up and played cricket with, so that they did not take me for an outsider. These were suspicious times, and strangers were not welcome in Guptanagar. Groups of tired men and women would be sitting in semicircles at the entrance to their homes and debating the riot. They would become quiet as they noticed a large, awkward body approach them. They would turn their heads and keep staring at me. One or two of them would stand up, their bodies tense. I would immediately wave to the familiar faces. 'Hai, Robinbhai . . . Late as usual uh . . .' one of them would call out, and the incessant talking would start again. I would smile. 'You should come back before sunset,' another would add, reclining on a string cot and playing with his infant daughter. 'It's really not safe out there.' I would shrug my shoulders and walk on.

But that night I could not remain focused. 'Collective punishment? How can anyone believe in collective punishment in this age and time?' I was talking to myself. 'What is wrong with this fellow?' I mumbled on. I could see

Jayendrasinh's face in my head. He had become awkward and stiff. This was the first time that he had seen me lose my temper. I was thinking I should see less of him until the violence ebbed, when someone put his right palm on my chest. I looked up. He was a thin man barely out of his teens, with a bony face and bloodshot eyes. His mouth reeked of home-brewed liquor. He was holding a small metal pipe in his left hand. I froze. I did not know him. But one of my cricketer friends shouted out, 'Hey Jiga, let him go . . .'

Jiga was not sure. 'What if he is a Muslim?' he slurred and spat some of the liquor-laced spit on my face. I became acutely aware of my groin, my penis and its missing foreskin.

My friend stood up and pushed him away. 'You son of a donkey!' he scolded Jiga. 'Living here for so long and still don't know Robinbhai.' Jiga wobbled away into a dark alley. My friend looked at me and added, 'Sorry Robinbhai. It is just that we have to be a little careful these days. It isn't his fault totally . . .'

'I understand,' I said almost affectionately, when in fact I could not understand. There was no way that the Muslims could reach this slum even if they decided to charge down the Guptanagar road. What did they have to be careful of? What were they afraid of?

But there was one thing I did understand. Jayendrasinh must have reached home much before me. The Satellite area, where he lived, was under curfew for only the first three days of the riots. After that Jayendrasinh had driven home every evening as if nothing unusual was happening in the rest of the city. There were no drunks in that posh locality to stop him. And neither was the foreskin missing from his penis.

CHAPTER ELEVEN

I woke up next morning with a dull headache. My throat was dry. I had not slept properly, having woken up at least three times during the night for no reason.

Demons had spilled out of Jayendrasinh's mouth and entered my head. They were trying to pin me down by pushing at my chest, grabbing my balls and inspecting my penis. I had to create my own thousand-armed goddess to ward them off.

I sat up in bed, but the jolt only made the pain shoot through. Maybe if I slept a little . . . But I was afraid of starting arguments with Jayendrasinh all over again if I closed my eyes. Hot tea drifting down my throat would help. And clearly drafted arguments that would instil some guilt in Jayendrasinh. That would help too. I wanted him to feel guilty. I could not believe that he felt pride in the rioters.

So, as mother started reheating some of the already prepared tea, I took a paper and pen to work out my arguments. It was an extremely silent Sunday morning. The curfew had been lifted for a couple of hours. Very few people had ventured out. The silence had magnified the sounds of the birds and the squirrels in the garden, creating an invisible canopy of birdcalls and twitterings over the house. I tried to forget the headache and concentrated on the white sheet of paper in front of me.

'You have a choice between two things,' I scribbled. 'One is your hatred for Muslims. The other is respect for the law. Street justice has no room in a democratic state that sees the rule of law as one of its foundations. Street justice only has room in failed states and dictatorships. If you are ready to give up the rule of law, you have to be ready to give up a major chunk of your democratic freedoms as well. You have to give up your right to be free and succumb to a set of laws, which are bendable. And once you start bending laws they can be bent both ways—for you and against you—depending on who has the power to implement them and what favours the person at that given moment. You may be bending the law today. Someone else may bend it against you on another day. You have to decide what is more important—the rule of law or street justice and your hatred for Muslims. You have to decide whether you want to be governed by the rule of law or whether you want to be governed by fear. Because only dictators govern by fear. Only tyranny needs fear.'

'Dictatorship' sounded too big for what I wanted to say. After all there was still a handful of people who openly protested against the violence and what they called 'the government's complicity in the violence'. They were being threatened. They were even beaten up. But they were protesting openly. Something they would never have been able to do in a dictatorship. If I said 'semi-dictatorship', the punch was lost. I was lost. I gave up. I would go with dictatorship and see what happens.

There was another internal flaw in the argument. It

assumed that all those who had been killed were guilty of something. This had to be corrected. All those who had been killed after 28 February were innocent and were being punished for their religion. I sipped the tea and ran the hot cup across my aching temples. It felt good.

While I was pushing at Jayendrasinh's demons inside my head, the freelance photographer Sam Nariman Panthaky was pushing at a wall of policemen who stood between him and Juhapura that Sunday morning.

Sam is a Parsi but nothing about him is stereotypically Parsi except perhaps that he is a bachelor at forty, and can say the most unexpected things in the most unexpected places. Apart from that he is dark-skinned, of medium height with curly hair and a thin moustache. His terry-cotton pants and mostly chequered shirts help him to merge with any crowd. He is a Muslim among Muslims and a Hindu among Hindus. He takes full advantage of this to get close to dead bodies and grief. I still remember his photographs of severed limbs lying in the rubble in the aftermath of the earthquake. Or even the tight close-up portraits he had taken of a man who had drowned in the Sabarmati and his bloated, half-eaten body which had floated up near Sardar Bridge a couple days later. I had never seen such multicoloured skin on a human being before. Some people call him an ambulance chaser but I think he would take that as a compliment.

On that Sunday morning, Sam had heard that Muslims from Juhapura were likely to clash with Hindus from Vejalpur on the western border of the ghetto, barely two kilometres from where I sat fighting Jayendrasinh's demons. The air was tense. Both sides had heard rumours. The streets were silent. But it was just the kind of silence that made most people uncomfortable and Sam was feeling distinctly edgy. He wanted to find a spot from where he could get the best shots when the battle erupted.

Two police jeeps had been stationed at the T-junction where the Guptanagar road was connected to National Highway Eight. The police had orders to not let anyone get past them. Not Sam, nor the television crew that joined him later. Behind the jeeps was Juhapura. The men in the jeeps looked tired. They told Sam they were the only khaki uniforms between Juhapura and Guptanagar. 'They had been given orders not to move from the spot and not to let anyone pass by,' Sam told me later while narrating the nightmare that unfolded before him that morning.

'To dissuade us from going further they said that if we were attacked, they would only be able to fire from a distance and nothing more. Our only hope was a senior police official who was expected to arrive there with a convoy in a while. We could perhaps join him if we could convince him, we thought, and turned back.'

Sam and the television crew were moving away from Juhapura when they saw running men ahead of them near Pravin Nagar. There were clumping into an existing circular mass and forming a large, loose ball of flesh which was becoming tighter every minute. Bodies glistening in the sun made the mass look like a large, shiny metallic ball. It was rolling on ahead of Sam and the TV crew, and gravitating towards an invisible magnetic dot 300 metres from where I sat fighting Jayendrasinh's demons.

The midget demons were still slamming my skull from the

inside with minute sledgehammers but they seemed to be tiring. The headache was showing signs of subsiding and I was thinking of ways to send ripples of doubt into Jayendrasinh's static pond of certainties.

I took another sip of the hot tea and wrote, 'You seem to believe that all Muslims are violent, sub-human animals, who, as you say, deserve to die. But is there a difference between them and you? Haven't you displayed the capacity for equal if not more violence? I fear that you have become as sub-human and violent as you claim the Muslims to be. You have become what you hate. So who are you killing and defeating in these bloody street fights? Isn't it your own self?'

I wanted to create a room full of mirrors in which Jayendrasinh would feel he was standing alone, and his reflection was that of a Muslim, complete with a skullcap and a beard. He would stand surrounded by a thousand Muslims all of whom were nothing but a reflection of himself. I started feeling a little better.

Which is when Sam heard a loud blast. It wasn't gunfire. In the last month, he had heard enough gunshots to tell the crack of a rifle from the blast of a tear-gas propeller or a petrol bomb. Something had just been blown up. Black smoke started to billow out from within the metallic ball.

'From a distance I could tell they were dragging something. It was not very big and it was not fighting back.'

Sam and the TV crew froze, halfway between the police jeeps and the ball. They were less than 100 metres from where I sat fighting Jayendrasinh's demons.

The blast triggered an explosion of men. As if the men were born with the blast. They started tumbling out from every crevice of Guptanagar and Pravin Nagar. More bodies glistening in the sun. Some of them young with slim bodies. Others old with large potbellies, running towards something at a distance. The ball was becoming bigger, tighter. From between the gaps in it were emanating strange, unintelligible voices. After a while it stopped moving forward and acquired a rubbery quality, swaying sideways and backward, left and right.

'We knew something terrible was happening but there was no way of knowing what. We knew the men had caught hold of somebody, but we were too far away to make out who it was. They had encircled it completely.'

Sam remembers vividly the total absence of patrolling on the street that day. Police jeeps that normally scouted for troublemakers were missing. He could not tell whether it was intentional or a coincidence.

He turned away from the mob to try and see if he could locate the police standing at the T-junction. Perhaps he could signal them, he thought, when something blinded him in the corner of his right eye. Like mirrors reflecting the sun. Glistening swords. 'If we had approached them they would have killed us too,' he told me while recounting the incident. 'I put my camera away. I knew instinctively I would become the magnet if they saw the camera in my hand. So I stood there, helpless.'

One man broke away from the metallic ball and ran towards Sam and the TV crew. 'The boys won't listen to me,' he said. 'They are adamant. This is really bad . . . Do you have a mobile?' Sam and the TV crew looked at each other. 'Arre hurry up before something bad happens,' he added. 'I am a social worker. I want to save that woman . . . Call up the DCP.'

The cameraman in the crew had a mobile. He called up a senior police official who said he would be there as soon as possible. And then they waited. The social worker rushed back to the metallic ball.

Sam knew he was badly caught between the police jeeps and the angry mass that had coiled around an invisible prey. On both sides of the road were shops, mostly ramshackle warehouses of antique dealers who resold wooden furniture. Behind them was a labyrinth of narrow lanes and by-lanes that even I had not mastered despite having lived in Guptanagar for thirty years. Sam knew he had to stand there and hope that the circular mass did not make him the next target.

I, on the other hand, was starting to feel freer of Jayendrasinh's demons. The headache was just a pinprick in my left temple. I too had heard the blast that had startled Sam but it was not accompanied with running men outside my door. So I took a last sip of the hot tea and wrote, 'I find it hard to believe that every last standing Muslim is a brainwashed fundamentalist. Is it possible that fifteen million Muslims have come together to conspire against all Hindus? If you see, they too are humans with families and personal histories, they too are a thinking, feeling people who are grappling with their identity in a world that is changing. I believe that there are many moderate Muslims and their voice can flourish if it is allowed to . . . At present, all you may have achieved is deliver the Muslim community to the fundamentalist mullah on a platter. All they need is the smouldering embers of hate and fear to fan their conservative Islam with. And that is what you may have given them when you thought you were teaching them a lesson.'

Then something unexpected happened. The metallic ball collapsed into floating human pieces. The circular mass parted. The human dyke opened. As Sam put it, 'It was like a lotus opening slowly.'

The men had seen something that had forced them to relent. Maybe the senior police official had arrived with his forces. Instead it was just one man on a scooter. A podgy man wearing a green helmet mostly found on policemen, his khaki uniform hidden behind a black jacket, rode through very slowly, almost deliberately from amidst the opening. 'Hey, what's happening there?' Sam asked when he reached them, but the man only looked at him and drove on slowly without answering. Sam would later recognize him in other parts of the city when the riots were at their peak, riding in the same way, in and out of streets.

By the time Sam could turn his gaze from the scooter back to the men, the metallic ball had formed again and had regained its grasp on the invisible prey.

'The swords were bobbing up and down in the middle of the circle by then. All I could make out was a burning scooter. There were glistening white swords and there was black petrol smoke.'

Sam started to panic. He lost his patience and rushed to the two police jeeps standing at the T-junction. 'Why the hell won't you guys do something!' he said exasperated. 'Can't you see there is trouble there?' he screamed. 'Come on! Do something! Stop those men! What the hell do you get paid for?'

The policemen finally got into their jeeps almost reluctantly. 'Must be nothing,' one of them said, peeved at having to move and give up his favourite position of lying on the back seat with his feet on the driver's backrest. 'They must have brought something out of a shop and must be burning it. Nothing else . . .' he added casually.

But then the sirens started to ring. Sam was relieved. The senior police official had arrived. With him was a battalion of paramilitary forces. The body language of the policemen in the jeep became more urgent. As if they had been on high alert all the time. The metallic ball evaporated, melting into the slum on both sides of the road.

That was the first time Sam saw Geetaben's naked body lying on the tar.

He brought out his camera.

She lay face down in the sand by the tar road. Her left leg was curled in as if she was trying to crawl. Her outstretched left hand held on to her white bra. Her right leg was bloodstained and wore a delicate silver anklet. Her pink salwar kameez lay strewn beside her in rags.

Today, Sam's photograph seems unreal. The large, ungainly and naked body of a full-grown woman lying in the middle of a backdrop that I can recognize. That is what made everything so unreal. I could recognize the road, the sand, the nearby shops—only Geetaben's dead body seemed artificially superimposed. It must have been noon by the time Sam took the photograph as there are no shadows in the picture. Not of Geetaben, not of Sam, nor of the policemen who had arrived by then. Just the road and Geetaben's naked body. Nothing was left of her. Her dignity had been taken away with her undergarments, and her life was taken away by the swords that rained on her.

'Her body was swollen by the time we reached,' Sam said while showing me the photograph. 'I think they first stripped her, then killed her and then danced on her body as a finale. Perhaps that is what they were doing when we saw the bobbing swords. And perhaps that is why her body was swollen.'

'Do you really think they must have danced on her body?' I asked.

'I think that is what must have happened,' Sam added. 'How else do you explain such a swelling of the body? They could not have been dancing on Geetaben's burning scooter. It was only a matter of minutes in between her being killed and us reaching. From what I know, dead bodies don't swell up so quickly.'

On the other side of the road lay her Muslim husband, his shirt full of blood. The mob had left him thinking he was dead, when he was in fact alive.

The senior police official, dressed in full uniform, was angry. 'Cover that body *now!*' he shouted at the constables, who had till then been gaping at Geetaben in disbelief. They didn't know how to respond. They seemed shocked. No one had a piece of cloth big enough to cover Geetaben's body. They tried covering her with her own pink salwar kameez, but it was too badly torn to cover her exposed flesh.

'I want the bastards who did this!' the senior official shouted at his men and they started running into the lane and by-lanes of Guptanagar.

'You know why they killed her?' Sam asked me after

returning the photograph into his camera bag.

'I think I do,' I said. 'Because she was a Hindu married to a Muslim man. But who were the men who killed her?' I asked, hoping he would say they were outsiders, not people I knew in Guptanagar.

'You know that thin, snaking slum next to the fields?' he asked.

'Yes,' I said. This was the last thing I wanted to hear. It had been my way home for almost a month now.

That evening Jayendrasinh called me on my mobile. After apologizing for his 'bandia bullshit' he asked, 'Is it true what I am hearing about Guptanagar?'

'What are you hearing?'

'That they stripped and murdered a woman?'

'Yes.'

'They actually stripped her in broad daylight in the middle of the road?'

'Do you want graphic details?'

'That is bad . . .'

Remorse? From Jayendrasinh? Could this one incident convert him and bring him on to my side? I was not sure. I asked, 'What is bad?'

'No, I mean the killing is all right but they should not have stripped her . . .'

'Excuse me?'

'Killing someone is one thing, stripping is another. They should not have stripped her. That is bad.'

'Please explain this to my rather naive brain. How is murder a lesser sin than stripping?'

'That is how many people feel. They feel awkward about

a woman being stripped in broad daylight, but they feel no guilt about the fact that she was later killed,' Sam had said.

I was left bewildered. I was living with people who believed killing was more acceptable than stripping. I have never been able to create this scale inside me where killing got more points than stripping.

Dinner was awkward that evening. Mother had forgotten to light the Shabbat candle on Friday after sundown and, following the extremely flexible Halacha of the David family, lit it on Sunday evening instead. Normally mother would start to relax under the yellow glow of the candle and a few sips of the port wine she kept hidden behind layers of books on the shelf in the living room. She would talk about everything, from how she missed Kiran's babbling to how the curfew and the forced isolation were starting to get to her. 'I mean, you know, thank god there is Ora,' she would say. 'She chases squirrels while I walk in the garden to rid myself of the Six o'clock Syndrome . . . Look I am even starting to lose weight with all that walking,' she would add, pulling in her paunch, and then smile.

But that evening she quietly served the tilkut ke batate pe anda (dry potato subzi topped with a fried egg) dinner and sat down in front of me nibbling at her food.

'Something wrong, mother?' I asked.

'Forget it,' she said staring at the fried egg on her plate. 'You will say I am paranoid.'

'I will not say anything,' I assured her. 'Tell me.'

'I heard about that murder near Pravin Nagar,' she said still staring at the fried egg. 'Did they really strip her?' she asked and looked at me directly for the first time that evening.

I wished I had an alternative answer but I didn't. So I said, 'Yes.'

'And then they killed her,' she asked.

'Yes.'

'What, Robin . . . How can you go to office every day and leave me alone here when people are being stripped and murdered in our backyard?' she asked, her tone moving from helplessness to frustration and anger. 'How many times do I have to tell you we can't live here? Is it just my responsibility to find a new house? You are the one who is going out every day. And you haven't gone and looked at one place. Not one place! I at least went to the Swaminarayan Avenue . . .'

'Mom, we can't rush into things like these,' I said, trying to remain calm. 'Where are we going to get seven–eight lakhs to buy a new house? We have to sell this house first. Besides, no one is going to hurt you here . . . No one will touch you.'

'Are you sure?' she asked, her eyes filled with defiance.

I looked at her. 'What?' I asked, hitting back with equal defiance, unable to understand what was making her so angry.

'You know I tried to go out yesterday evening . . . The Six o'clock Syndrome was killing me. So I took the slum road that you take to try and go to CG Road or some place . . .'

'You didn't tell me.'

'Well, whatever. And you know what happened? Boys ran after me shouting bibdi . . . bibdi . . . They thought I was Muslim because I was wearing parallel pyjamas under my kurta . . . And within seconds there was a large crowd behind me. There were men and women and children all looking at me suspiciously.'

Goose pimples started to form on my hands and legs. I

could see mother with her flowing mane of white hair, red kurta and parallel pyjamas helplessly standing before a swarm of angry, sunburnt bodies. 'But didn't they see your chandla?' Mother always anointed her forehead with a large red dot before leaving home, and most people thought she was Hindu.

'I had covered my head with a dupatta. Of course they went away once I removed it, and they saw the chandla. I didn't think much of this until I heard about Geetaben but it can be me tomorrow, Robin . . . It can be me . . .'

'Mom, they know you,' I said feebly. I didn't know what to say to console her. 'They won't touch you,' I added almost apologetically.

'Don't be naive,' she said and banged the fork on the table. 'Do you really think they did not know Geetaben? For God's sake, Robin!'

I kept looking at her, fiddling with the fork in my hand. According to me it was the people you loved and hated. Not the clothes they garbed themselves in. Obviously I was wrong.

After a while she said, 'Sometimes I wonder why we came back from Israel. We should have stuck it out there. We should have stuck it out.'

The silence in Guptanagar was unbearable after that.

CHAPTER TWELVE

The shadow of the flying kite glided past on the empty road. Its silent movement startled me. The bird was making no effort to fly. The weight of the wind under its outstretched wings was allowing it to float and create a beautiful, black crescent that singed the asphalt. As it drew large, invisible circles in the sky, its shadow appeared and disappeared from the range of my sight.

This was the first time I had seen the shadow of a flying bird so clearly. But then never before had the main Guptanagar road been so empty at midday, allowing shadows to float. Speeding cars, defecating cows, slow-moving camel carts and a continuous stream of men, women and children had trampled all over the shadows until now. Until the curfew.

The drifting crescent reminded me of mother's short poem about birds of prey.

The last Kesuda had bled its heart out in this month of March,
High above the vultures are flying,
Moving backwards and forwards forming a triangle.
Have they spotted the mark of fresh blood
Or are they the cranes searching for a landing
Before the night of the return?

Mother had written these words when we had decided to return from Israel after our second failed attempt. She was afraid people would make fun of her, or make faces and say, 'You are like that only . . .'

Ever since Geetaben's murder, an indefinite curfew had been clamped on the road. Nothing moved but the occasional patrolling police jeep, the wind lifting clouds of dust from the roadside and the flying kite.

I had also stopped taking the back road through the slum. My friends, who had saved me from Jiga and his kind, still greeted me, but I had felt awkward the few times I had gone that way. The thought that I had been sitting comfortably at my dining table, conjuring hypothetical arguments and sipping tea while a woman was being stripped and murdered so close to home made me feel like a helpless coward. True, I had not been aware of the incident, but would that have made a difference? Would I have been able to help had I been in Sam's place? The question drifted in and out of my head incessantly. I fear I would have been more frozen than Sam. It is likely that I would not have known what to do. And now there was nothing to do except take the only other route, the main road, ignore my guilt and admire the crescent shadow of a flying bird.

Before the curfew had been clamped, this fifteen-feet-broad road had hummed so loudly with the thick current of traffic that it had drowned everything else. This was the tail end of the municipal corporation limits which connected to National Highway Number Eight—one of the busiest highways in the country—connecting Gujarat to Mumbai. People and things entered and left the city from here in such a constant stream that you wished you had a magic wand that could split this Red Sea traffic. But that was before the train was burnt at Godhra.

As I walked on towards Anjali Char Rasta, police jeeps and the army convoys looked at me with suspicion. I brought out my curfew pass and they let me go. In between, there was nothing but silence marked by the sound of my own footsteps, stray dogs scratching their ears, sparrows invisibly twittering in trees and boys playing cricket in narrow lanes somewhere behind garish posters on deadpan walls. Their occasional cheers gave the sense that life was not too far away.

Had it not been for the curfew the stray dogs would not have noticed me. But now they took a keen interest and approached me very slowly as if stalking me. I could see policemen with loaded rifles looking at me suspiciously from behind a curtain of fine dust. So I couldn't even pick up a stone and fling it at the dogs. Lifting a stone on a curfew-bound street could easily be misunderstood by the policemen. They could take me for a rioter. I ignored the dogs in the hope that at some point they would ignore me too.

I was still keeping one eye on the dogs behind my right shoulder, when the rattle of a broken piece of asbestos hanging from a shut garage and swaying with the wind made me jump. I turned around and a wall of dust lifted by the wind slammed into my face.

My head was swirling in a broth of strange memories. Dust and that day in Israel when I stood at the edge of the field transfixed by a helicopter. The helicopter that looked like the peacock feather I carried inside me. The peacock feather and my dream of falling and floating. The dream and the earthquake. The earthquake and my large, hemiplegic body. My body and Manali, the woman I had once considered settling down with. Manali and our peaceful walks on Nehru Bridge over the trickle of the Sabarmati River.

I believe the broth is cooked by the fine riverbed dust.

In fact, had it not been for the pushy afternoon wind, the Sabarmati would have remained just a snaking sandpit in Ahmedabad's blistering summers. Bone-dry and curling like a python lying limp, heavy with the burden of a large prey in its belly.

The wind ensures that this python crawls. It drags the abundant dust on the riverbed into the uneven skyline along both banks, resembling the shattered teeth of a retired street brawler. Black and broken.

Like a predator slave to its instinct to hunt, the python scales the muddy walls of the banks gingerly, as if stalking a careless victim. It coils around old, broken homes, all set to grip them in its deathly embrace, but remembers the prey in its belly, changes its mind and moves on.

Once in the city, the serpentine wind gathers the momentum of a thousand pythons and slaps your face with the dust. As if someone had clutched the head of the snake in a firm, muscular grasp, but left the tail free to swing wildly and hit anything that came in its way.

The slap ensures that the dust enters your nostrils, lines your lungs and flows into your black bloodstream. Like nicotine.

In fact the Sabarmati died many years back, but the loo refused to let go of it. It decided to keep it alive by uniting it with the only other large body of liquid available in Ahmedabad, the collective bloodstream of its people. And now it moves with the people, lives with the people and dies with the people, only to be born again and to die again, all the time moving on dry earth, sheathed in flesh and bone.

For all its force, however, the birth of this river-rejuvenating wind is an agonizingly slow process. It takes place in the womb of summer afternoons. The deadly trident of a blinding white sun, a cloudless sky of thin blue and forty-five degrees of burning Centigrade unite to father it in the stillness of dawn. The union stabs to death the last remains of the cool freshness of the beginning of the day and then becomes even more powerful. The white sun turns whiter still, taking away the few drops of blue left in the sky. The heat begins to soar. Like slow poison. You can't feel it crawl in your veins, but it is numbing you. Slowly. The afternoon has begun. The wind is born.

When everything has slowed down to the speed of time, and the senses can't perceive the pace of change, the wind begins its forward march, injects life into the limp python and lifts it from the riverbed and into the city.

The evenings take away the sun and the snake, but not before it spits out five million people from its nauseous belly—their thin-walled homes.

Their trampling kicks up another sandstorm, but a gentle one this time. As if each crystal of dust were a butterfly with silken wings, soundlessly floating in the city. A thick blanket rises over the city's horizon in slow motion. The dust glides and gently caresses everything. Eyelashes. Dry lips. Sweaty necks. The insides of uncut nails. Navels. Nostrils.

When every crevice in the city has had its fill of dust and the collective broad shoulders of the million miniature storms start to droop, unable to empty their burden, the earth trembles. As if Atlas has malaria. Everything shakes, moves, trembles, breaks.

The earthquake strikes. An untimely monsoon. A dark, waterless mass gathers under our feet noticed by no one. We are used to scanning the skies for the first hint of the clouds, heavy with rain, but not under our feet.

But it gathers. First in lines of thin grey, each collapsing into the singular mass of black with no silver lining and dense like the moonless amavasya. A gentle drizzle begins. There are no diamond-shaped droplets of water in this shower. Just movement. Thick, wavy blobs of movement.

This is Ahmedabad's first monsoon of movement. A short burst of forty-five seconds and the earth turns liquid. A separate set of laws takes over. The dark cloud releases its burden by letting loose flowing wrath. Everything begins to float in the rising tide of this flashflood of movement. People, things, homes, beliefs, certainty. Everything. A powerful forward thrust lifts them up to the crest of the wave. And then they rush down towards the trough, crashing like drunken slalom skiers rolling downhill. Out of control.

Wave after wave follows, lifting up and flinging down all that was permanent and all that was transient. Even homes built only the year before and standing with their chests jutting out, as if saying, 'Dare me,' collapse. The wave had the force to uproot them from their foundations and then simply leave them in mid-air, to watch them fall, crumble and disintegrate in the descent to the trough.

And then midway through its climb to the crest, the wave disappears. But that was not the end of the monsoon of movement. From the incomplete end of the wave a whirlpool formed. A quick, circular turn of the earth destined to complete a 180-degree turn and bring down all that was left standing from the onslaught of the wave. But at about 120 degrees the monsoon decided to abate and peter out, leaving everything cracked and full of crevices.

Like a forgotten 100-year-old seed embedded in the earth that never lost its desire to sprout, cracks and crevices burst out from it with the force of a million leafless neem trees yawning out after a deep slumber undisturbed by nightmares. First, they appear at the foundations of the homes, like an army of worker ants assembling in crooked columns before attacking the agenda of the day. And then suddenly they start crawling on to the virgin walls, climbing to the top.

Sometimes I wished that the wind would stand still, that the butterfly wings would melt away on the dust, allowing this blanket to freeze in mid-air. It would create a thick but pregnable wall of fine crystals. A wall that allowed you to chisel out shapes simply by nudging it in.

If I were to walk through this wall, my body would punch its outline in it. Like anti-matter, it would chisel out my silhouette in emptiness.

It would be the world's first mirror of dust clearly reflecting the confused outline of my body. A mirror that carves the left outline with the precise proportions of a man who stands five feet eleven inches and weighs eighty kilos. For the right, however, it reflects the outline of a much smaller body. Someone who is barely five feet five inches and weighs ten kilos less—as if it had a completely different person in mind. As if two different halves from two different bodies have been forcibly fused into one, giving birth to an incongruity that rules my world.

Hemiplegia, they tell me it is called medically.

What the doctor did not say is that for the rest of my life my body would follow two separate time zones. The right side will trail behind the left. When the finger on my left palm twitches, the right will only understand sensation. When the left palm grabs, the right will barely twitch.

I am exposed.

The only incongruity this mirror does not reflect is the streaks of white in my mop of black hair. Like the thin rivers of melting snow I have seen on mountain caps from the bottom of the Jordan Valley. At thirty, this mesh of black-and-white hair is not congruent with my large, chubby face.

Sometimes I feel my body has been incongruously designed to remind me that I am a stranger wherever I go, whatever I do. The gentle beginnings of my incongruity are made just below my bushy black eyebrows, in my eyes. As if the floodgates have just been opened and the slight trickle down the thick walls can only be a precursor to an impending flash flood.

My right eyeball prefers to kiss the bridge of my nose. I find it difficult to hold it in the centre despite three surgeries. They call it a squint. Or look-London-turn-Tokyo. Or a walking-talking joke.

So I try to hide it with my spectacles, hoping that that the outside world will be reflected on the glass. Hoping that the blur of images, like a film in fast forward, will distract anyone trying to make eyeball-to-eyeball contact. I think it works.

But not always. Like it did not work for Manali's mother. Despite years of practice at disguising the squint, never taking off my glasses in public and never looking directly into the eyes of people who did not know me well, I could not fool her. She had noticed the visual aberration and ticked off her daughter for her bad taste.

Manali told me of her decision to leave me in the best way she could. Here is what she said:

'I have to tell you something,' she had said while we were sitting on the Freudian couch in the living room by the window. I was caressing her soft hair and kissing her right ear.

'Now?' I had said. I loved playing with her hair.

'I told mom we are together,' she said and looked at me with cold eyes.

I took my hand out of her hair and said, 'Why did you have to do that?'

'I don't know,' she said awkwardly, took my left hand into her palms and started playing with my fingers nervously as if she was counting them.

'What do you mean you don't know? Didn't we talk about this? Didn't we decide to hold back till we are both ready to face the storm she will unleash?' I asked.

'Look, she coaxed it out of me . . .' she said, her voice barely audible.

'Coaxed it out of you?' I took my hand out of hers. 'How old are you? Six?'

(Silence)

'And I suppose she gave you a long list of reasons for not seeing me, right?'

'Right.'

'Brilliant. And what is her main objection? That I am Jewish I suppose . . . In more than a billion people in this wide nation you had to find yourself a Jew . . .'

'Well, if you have to know, that doesn't bother her at all.'

'Then what?'

(Silence)

'Don't tell me it's my family tree. Hindu father, Jewish mother . . . Divorced. All that . . .'

'Can you stop speculating? It's not that. I am going through hell right now and I don't need more of it. I don't have to handle two hells at the same time . . .'

'Then let me tell you my love, I think I know what it is. It's my crooked body. I am not the perfect bridegroom for her perfect daughter. I mean, imagine what your relatives will say . . . That you married a handicapped man and a Jew on top of that . . . How totally marginalized can you get?'

'Look, stop or I am leaving.'

'Actually, I can understand her. Who would want an album full of marriage photos of your pretty daughter standing next to a man with a squint in one eye?'

'Will you shut up?'

'Not before you tell me what you think. Are you going to listen to your mother?'

'I don't know what to think.'

'Are you going to listen to your mother, or not?'

'Look, it's not just my mother. It's my family. I have been to hell with them and back . . .'

'Are you going to listen to your mother, or not?'

(Silence)

(Silence)

'Have you seen my cousin with the funny walk? You know, the break dance thing he does . . .'

Hmm.

'He has congenital rheumatoid arthritis. I have often wondered how they are going to find him a so-called normal bride . . .'

(Silence)

(Silence)

The squint, however, is only a part of my many aberrations. God gave me this gift of being monocular. This means I can see through only one eye. The left one. I can't see an object sitting on the edge of my right eye. It is my blind spot. Just like the blind spot in my brain that refuses to store dreams.

The result is I have lived more on the left side of the world. The left side is more real. More matter. Less magic.

The right side has always been a perception of the left. A messy mix of half-seen visions, half-touched objects, half-fondled breasts, half-experienced pleasures, only a dim sensation of pain.

But a full understanding of my incongruity.

■

A grey cloud of pigeons suddenly shot out from the black Hajam Mojam dome in a flurry of flapping wings.

'Hai madarchod! Where do you think you are going!' a policeman was shouting and slowly running behind me, his rifle in one hand and a cane in the other. I pulled out my curfew pass just before he reached striking distance. 'Press,'

I shouted as loud as I could, but felt as if dust was stuck in my throat. I cleared it and strained again with another, 'Press bhai, press.'

'So why couldn't you have told me that before?' He was angry. I could see the tense nerves of his right forehand, which was holding the cane. 'Do I have to shout ten times before you can hear me, or you think you can get away with anything because you are the fucking press?'

'No, no, I was just . . .' I was about to say I was thinking about something, but it sounded stupid on a curfew-bound street. You can't tell a policeman about walls of dust and former girlfriends when he has come close to beating you up. So I said, 'It won't happen again.'

'You can thank your lord I am not in a bad mood,' he said as he started moving back to his post near the Hajam Mojam. 'You can thank your lord it was me. Had it been the army, they would have broken your legs first and then asked for your pass.'

I slapped my forehead and started walking towards Anjali Char Rasta. I saw a cloud of fine dust mushrooming out of my ears for the second time in my life that day. Strange things the silence of the curfew does to your head.

CHAPTER THIRTEEN

You cannot live in row houses if your family is in the habit of loud, uproarious brawls and screaming fits of temper. The walls of these concrete blocks, standing shoulder to shoulder, row after row, are too thin and your neighbours too close for you to indulge in an extremely personal and nasty attack on a family member and believe that it will remain between the two of you. It is bound to travel in muffled but audible tones in all directions. If you can't control your temper, nothing remains personal and private here. As if the walls of the home are built of a thousand ears of neighbours which twist and follow you everywhere you go. As if they are whispering to each other in conspiring tones, 'You know, he said this and this to his mother . . . Can you believe it? Mother and son talking like this and at the top of their voices, that too . . .'

'Scream, and be stripped of your privacy' an invisible sign seemed to say as mother and I stepped into the old row house behind the famous lotus-shaped temple Manav Mandir on the way to the drive-in theatre. After Geetaben's murder this was one of the first homes that we had decided to look at as a possible new home, to get away from the memory of a dead, naked woman lying in the middle of a road at noon.

Geetaben's murder was only a week old. Mother and I had fought over my lethargy to help find another home. She had accused me of living only between office and lolling around on the Freudian couch watching 'silly shit like *Xena the Warrior Princess*' on television.

She was not completely wrong but I was not ready to relent. I said that the silly shit was needed to relax. 'Mom my head will explode if I don't relax,' I told her. 'Silly shit on television is very good to forget the silly shit we are living in.'

'And where am I supposed to go and relax?' she asked angrily, her arms akimbo, standing next to the dining table as I gulped down lunch in a hurry to go to office. 'You at least get out of the house, meet people, all that . . . I am stuck here day after day . . . The only people I see are the maids and the men running in front of the house with swords in their hands.'

'Ma, don't start with me right now,' I said, not looking at her. 'I have a lot of things to do today. And don't make it sound as if it is a crime to watch television and relax.'

'Yes, yes, you will have a lot of time to relax after I am dead . . .' she said in a fit of temper, and set into motion a loud avalanche of arguments in which I accused her of never understanding me and she accused me of not understanding the gravity of the situation and escaping facts by running to office. Of course from there, the arguments moved to how I never let her say what she really felt, always butting in with a, 'Please . . . not right now!' and how she always complained about everything and a lot of other things that are best kept behind the walls of the Guptanagar home. Although, I suspect that anyone who passed by the house that day knows exactly what we had to say to one another. We were so loud.

By the end of the day, however, we had tracked down the phone number of a property broker who dealt exclusively in the Drive-In and Manav Mandir areas ahead of Satellite, where no one even vaguely worried about the presence of Muslims, or Geetabens or curfews. The city moved and hummed. People walked and talked. Children played on the streets. As if the riots were nothing more than television images, as unreal as *Xena the Warrior Princess*.

'A little old I accept, madam, but then this is the best you can get if you are looking for a small garden to keep your dog in,' said Jayanti Pathak, the broker, a short, thin man with a thin moustache. He was standing in the empty living room which had dark-pink walls, closed windows with opaque grey glass, a musty stench and a thick layer of dust everywhere. Ora had charged at Pathak when he tried to enter the Guptanagar home during a break in the curfew to make the initial contact. She had developed an instant dislike for the man and I had had to hold on to her for as long as he was in the house. She had kept growling softly from the belly all the while. Mother had let him know that whatever home we bought would need to have a place for Ora, which was one reason we had started with the row house.

Inside the row house, mother was buzzing around while I stood at the entrance, screwing up my face to let her know that I did not like the place. Everything seemed claustrophobic—the mosaic floors, the pink walls, the narrow staircase from the living room leading to the bedrooms on the first floor, the kitchen, which was half as big as the one in Guptanagar, and of course the thin walls.

Someone flushed a toilet in the house on the left. On the right, a television set blared with a fight between a mother-in-law and daughter-in-law, interspersed with background music that signified impending disaster. There were other sounds—the clink of glasses, muffled laughter, children fighting over a toy . . . If I shouted in the living room, at least two houses in either direction would have a clear idea of what I was angry about.

I stepped out into the small, concrete, square-shaped courtyard in the front of the row house. There was a champa tree, a thin bougainvillea creeper and a tulsi shrub in the centre. The low gate opened into a narrow gangway, which connected all the other row houses. I looked around to make eye contact with neighbours I had only heard so far, and saw row after row of identical courtyards with the odd human figure floating in and out, each with one champa, one thin bougainvillea and one tulsi, and a small gate connecting the gangway. The only difference would be in the density of the bougainvillea creeper or in the number of flowers that had blossomed on the champa tree. There were similar rows in front and many more behind.

This was a machine-produced world in which you were expected to fit in like a small, mass-produced cog, turning silently in one direction day after day, year after year. Symmetry and indistinguishable uniformity were the norms.

Mother came out of the row house. Pathak followed her, fidgeting with the keys. 'What do you think?' she asked. I shrugged my shoulders. She turned around and surveyed the courtyard and then asked, 'Will Ora fit into this much? I mean she is used to much more . . .'

'Will we fit into this?' I asked. 'I mean *we* are used to much more . . .'

'We will have to make a compromise somewhere no, Robin . . .' she said and turned to Pathak. 'How much is it for?' she asked.

'Slightly expensive, madam,' he said, 'about fifteen lakh rupees. But if you are serious then, you know, I can always ask the owner to bring down the price a touch. Plus, like I told you, we can always arrange for finance . . . A bank loan. Whatever suits you . . .'

'Robin, we will have to sell our house first.' Mother looked at me and said, 'I am scared of loans . . .'

I shook my head vertically and looked away. I have never understood matters of money and real estate. In fact I get panic attacks each time I am made to sign many legal documents. To the extent that the pen starts to wobble and I find it difficult to maintain a uniform signature.

'And I would appreciate it if you showed some interest in all this,' she added sarcastically.

'But I am showing interest,' I said feebly as we started walking out of the society gate and Pathak was locking all the doors of the row house. 'Did you like the house?'

'It is a little crummy no . . .' she said. 'Very little space compared to our garden, but then we have to think about Ora . . .'

'We have to think about ourselves, not Ora,' I said. 'Ora will have to adjust to whatever we choose.'

'Yes, yes, but I think I will be happy on the ground floor somewhere. Flats frighten me,' she said in a more relaxed manner now that she had opened up a conversation with me.

'Mom, fifteen–sixteen lakhs is not the kind of money we have . . . We have to at least look at a flat. What are you afraid of? The lack of privacy?' I asked.

Mother mumbled something I could not hear. So I asked her again, 'What did you say?'

'I am afraid of the earthquake,' she finally said, her voice barely audible above the traffic as we walked towards Pathak's office in a shopping centre nearby.

'Earthquake?' I was not sure I had heard her right.

She kept walking silently.

'Which earthquake?' I asked. 'The one that is already forgotten or the one that you think may occur in the future?'

There was a hint of sarcasm in my voice but she did not respond to it. 'Is there a difference?' she asked. We were holding a conversation in questions.

'What do you mean?' I asked.

'No, no, what if there is an earthquake and we are stuck on some top floor?'

The earthquake had been the last thing on my mind in months but mother seemed to have carried it in her all the time.

Mother saw the bewilderment on my face, and added, 'No, I will look at the flats but I don't want to go too high. I don't want to go beyond the first or second floor. It's better if we can find a tenement or something. It will be better for Ora also.'

Pathak went on to show us some flats in a massive complex of hundreds of homes that day, not too far away from the row houses. So many people lived so close to each other here that it was easy to imagine them as part of one giant organism from which little, secluded pieces had broken away and then joined back in. On each floor of these eight-storey giants there were four flats, each opening into a small landing and a lift with a sliding grill. There was a constant stream of people going up and down, right and left, rubbing shoulders, shaking hands, saying *'Kem chho?'* The lift never seemed to stop, constantly carrying people and making an odd, rickety sound. The landing between floors was so small that if five people came on to it at the same time, they would involuntarily kiss each other. And each floor had a different sound and a different fragrance wafting from the kitchens—dal being prepared in kokam juice, sambhar masala boiling on the gas stove, a huge blob of ghee melting in sooji for sheera.

Many of the doors were forever open. You could peep into the privacy of people's homes and they did not object, lazing around on expensive, gaudy furniture or squatting on the floor. In almost every home the television set was constantly blaring Hindi film songs, sitcoms, roaring volcanoes, the hee-haw of Hong Kong karate movies and the signature tunes of twenty-four-hour television channels. I was used to living in a house where I could control the sounds and fragrances that entered. Of course there were times when the stench of a dead stray dog rotting in the fields or the stinging smoke of tear gas would fill our senses for hours. Or a bhajan session would go on till 4 a.m. with the loudspeaker so loud that you felt the singer was sitting on your bed and trying to serenade you with his hoarse voice. But that was rare. It happened once in a while. Not like this. People walking in and out of your hair as if they had infested your scalp.

'What are these, pigeonholes?' I asked. I had not lived so close to so many people for a long time. It seemed as if we were constantly pushing at a wall of humans threatening to close in.

Pathak could tell I did not like the place and tried to say something, but mother came to his rescue. 'No, no, let's look at the place at least, Robin,' she said. 'Maybe the insides are nicer. Besides, there are so many people, I will not feel lonely if you are not around.'

'There are many other advantages also, madam,' Pathak added quickly before I could say anything. 'This is a very cosmopolitan place. You can cook maas, macchi, everything and no one will say anything. And there are all kinds of people here, Gujaratis, non-Gujaratis, Christians . . . You will be very comfortable.'

'How many Muslims?' I asked.

He looked shocked. 'Muslims? No, no . . . No Muslims here,' he said but then saw the smirk on my face and started smiling. 'You are teasing me. You know there are no Muslims here. There is never any tension here . . . You know we had curfew only for the first day here when it all started.' He was referring to the riot. That is how people referred to the violence here. 'It'.

'So how can you call this place cosmopolitan if there are no Muslims?' I wanted to ask. But I didn't. I knew that for him being able to cook mutton and chicken in the privacy of your kitchen, without your neighbours complaining about the wafting fragrance, was cosmopolitan enough. You could not ask for more. A place would become 'communal' if there were Muslims living nearby, not 'cosmopolitan'.

Our first flat was on the fourth floor, where one H.P. Gandhi had broken down the wall between two flats and made it into a sprawling place with a huge living room, opening into smaller bedrooms and a kitchen. There was cheap grey marble flooring and sparkling white walls with amateur watercolour landscapes that looked like bad imitations.

'We are immigrating to Australia,' Gandhi told us as we sat down for a formal glass of Coke after an initial survey of the rooms. His forehead was anointed with a yellow paste and pictures of gods and goddesses anointed the otherwise empty walls. There was minimal furniture. Just a handful of chairs and a dining table. 'We had applied almost two years back. Finally got all our papers,' he added, his voice resounding in the empty rooms. The rest of the family, made up mainly of women, preferred to stay in the kitchen, peeping once in a while from behind the curtain. Gandhi looked like a man who followed a strict regime. His athletic frame suggested that he exercised regularly, and his trimmed moustache and his pitch-black hair with grey at the fringes that he spent a lot of time in front of the mirror. Sitting cross-legged and relaxed on a plastic garden chair, Gandhi showed no signs of anxiety about starting a new life at such a late age. Quite the opposite of the mad frenzy we had kicked up before leaving for Israel. He said he was a senior official in the excise department and had saved up enough to go to Australia and start a small business.

Mother and I were about to ask him the price of the flat when he asked, 'So are you Roman Catholic or Protestant?'

Mother looked at me awkwardly and smiled. 'Actually . . . we are Jews,' I said.

'You are what?' he asked.

'Jews,' mother said. 'You know . . . Yahudis. We are different.'

'I know the Jews,' he said, as if he was hurt at us assuming that he did not know the Jews. 'One of my colleagues in the excise department was Jewish. Nice man . . . In fact I am a great admirer of the Israelis. Surrounded by Muslims on three sides and nothing but deep sea on the fourth, and yet look at them . . . No one dare touch them. That is what I call courage.' His face glowed with admiration.

We nodded politely. We would have preferred to ask him about water supply, sewage connections and the number of ceiling fans he was planning to leave behind, apart from the price he expected. But then he was making small talk and we did not want to seem rude.

'In fact India should learn a thing or two from these Israelis, I tell you,' he went on. 'We can solve half our problems that way.'

I was not sure if he was talking about drip irrigation or bombing entire localities in Palestine-controlled areas while retaliating against terrorists.

Again an awkward moment of silence. We did not know whether to continue with the small talk or come to the point. 'So it must be hard living so close to the border. The curfew and all that . . .' The conversation was going in the direction that we did not want it to go. 'How did decent people like you get stuck in a place like Guptanagar?' Pathak must have told him about us. But before we could answer, he added, 'I tell you these Muslims will never learn.'

Mother and I nodded again and I changed the topic, 'So when are you planning to leave for Australia?'

'Oh, in a week,' he said. 'All the formalities are over. We are planning to set up a grocery store near Melbourne. Yow know we are doing all this for our children. They will have a better . . .'

Mother was growing increasingly impatient. She must have been reminded of our failed attempts at immigrating to Israel and seemed uncomfortable with the ease with which the man was taking such a huge step in life. She interrupted him with, 'Very nice, very nice, and how much do you expect for the house?'

'Well, twelve lakhs, but we can negotiate,' he said. 'You people seem nice and money is not too much of a concern for me. I have already sold another of my flats, so don't worry. You can even pay me in instalments if you want.'

As we got up to leave, mother noticed that the wall near the entrance had been whitewashed comparatively recently. It had been repainted. Underneath it there was a thin bulge like a bandage running diagonally across the wall from left to right. 'What happened here?' she asked Gandhi.

'Oh, nothing,' he said. 'Just a small crack. A remnant of the earthquake. Very superficial. Don't worry, it's not structural.'

Mother touched the bulge and turned around. 'Mr Pathak—'

'Absolutely nothing to worry,' Pathak said before mother

could say anything more. 'Would I show you a house that was earthquake damaged? I have to survive in this business, madam, don't worry . . .'

Mother started scratching her head once we came out of the flat. 'Mr Pathak, all this twelve lakhs and fifteen lakhs is too much for me,' she said a little irritated with the broker. 'And that too earthquake affected. I told you my budget is five–six lakhs which can be stretched to seven. Not more.'

'But madam you only said you wanted a slightly larger place where you can keep your dog. So these were the only two that I thought were large enough. And I have also seen the number of things you have in your house. Besides, I am telling you don't worry about the price. I will arrange for all the finance.'

'It is easy for you to say "Don't worry about the finance,"' mother seemed to be getting more irritated. 'Plus, that crack . . .'

'Mom, let us first look at the places and then we will decide,' I said. 'And you know he does have a point. You can't buy a second-hand house that is completely free of cracks after the earthquake.'

'No, no, I am not moving into a house that is even slightly damaged,' she said, gesticulating angrily. 'Nothing doing.'

'But mother . . .' I tried to placate her but it had the opposite effect.

'What do you want me to do?' Mother's temper and voice were rising now. 'Go from earthquake to riot to earthquake again? Are you out of your mind? Have you forgotten how much those cracks had frightened me?'

Pathak looked nonplussed. It was obvious he had not seen such public display of anger before. I had, and did not argue any further. That was the only way to quieten her. Anything could have triggered her temper. It could have been the price of the flat. It could have been that crack on the wall that everyone else except her seemed to be taking in their stride. It could have been the memory of the failed immigration attempts to Israel triggered off by Gandhi. It could have been any or all three of them bundled into one. And anything I said would only make it worse.

There was a brief silence and then she told Pathak, her voice sounding edgy, 'And what is all this loan-shoan business? I have never carried the burden of a loan on my head before and I am not going to start now. Besides, who is going to give me a loan at this point? I am fifty-five and don't even have a job. What am I supposed to say on the loan papers? That I am a freelance writer who gets paid peanuts for the books I write?'

'Mom, I will take the loan if needed,' I said as calmly as possible, with my arm around her shoulder. 'Don't worry.'

'No, no, I think I will sell the Guptanagar house first,' she said firmly. 'I don't want to live in that house. Anyway I don't like that house too much.'

She thought she hated the house. That is what she thought.

CHAPTER FOURTEEN

Strange things started to happen after we decided to sell the house. Things that now seem like omens. But at that time they were just a string of unexplained occurrences.

First, the six neem trees surrounding the house, including my favourite one with the ibis perched at the top, dried up and died. They had turned into a network of bony and wrinkled arms twisted into each other, like frozen streaks of black lightning. They reminded me of the black-and-white ink drawings from my childhood, which had spilled out of the drawers of the table in my room during the earthquake. There was a time when it was difficult to see the sky from behind the dense green network of crisp little leaves that enveloped these branches when the trees were alive. But now the sky jutted out in uneven shapes of a complex jigsaw puzzle, which would take years to put together.

'Should do something about those drawers,' I would tell myself every day while climbing up the staircase leading to the balcony, but forget about them almost immediately. There were too many objects in those drawers that reminded me of unfinished business. The rusted guitar strings, for instance, reminded me of how I had never gone beyond strumming a handful of Beatles songs. The Hebrew dictionary that reminded me of Israel. Love letters that reminded me of women, some of whom I missed, others I was almost embarrassed to have been associated with.

When I had taught myself to dissociate the trees from the Memory Drawers, the squirrels in the garden started nibbling at the plastic mosquito netting on the window in the kitchen, finally cutting out a neat hole in it. Both mother and I were so engrossed in keeping a tab on the times at which curfew would be relaxed so that we could go out and find ourselves a house that we did not notice the hole at first. But then every evening after sunset the house would be full of mosquitoes, their buzzing magnified by the silence of the curfew, and their bites ensured that we slept badly.

It was mother who first noticed the hole and plugged it with thick, black scotch tape used by electricians to insulate live wire. We had taken the squirrel's nibbling as an aberration, which would not be repeated, and forgot about it after plugging the hole. But the flock of mynahs in the garden proved us wrong. The scotch tape seemed to attract the birds as they started attacking other parts of the netting, nosediving into it around the tape and softening it for the squirrels to nibble at. The mynahs were like black darts that appeared from behind the leaves, their beaks aimed straight at the netting.

Mother was reminded of Alfred Hitchcock's movie *Birds*. She would joke about it saying, 'Imagine! Being surrounded by bloodthirsty mynahs of all things at a time like this . . .' The fact is that of all the birds in the garden mother had never liked the mynahs. 'Have you seen the way they look at us?' she would ask. 'As if they don't care for us. I hate them.'

This dislike had something to do with the patch of bare yellow skin they had around their dark-red eyes, their loud, scolding chatter which sounded like *keek keek keek kok kok kok* and their absurd bobbing of the head.

'Look at them!' mother would say, exasperated after one of the mynahs had scored a hit, collapsed on to the window sill, flown away to a safe distance and then perched on one of the flower-laden branches of the champa tree in the neighbour's garden followed by the bobbing of the head. 'What defiance!'

Soon more birds started joining what had initially looked like the game of a few. And then mother started to worry. The birds would dart into the netting even while we were sitting on the table near the window, collapse on to the window sill by the impact and then fly off. On more than a couple of occasions I dropped boiling tea on myself, startled by the muffled thuds.

Our first defence against the perfectly aimed black darts was Ora. She was forced into spending more time in the garden in the hope that she would reclaim her territory and keep the birds away from the window. The dog had become used to spending her days indoors as mother needed her company while I was at work. And the mynahs had taken over the garden. Ora's occasional frenzied barking had no effect on them. They kept darting in at regular intervals. Muffled thuds could be heard from any part of the house, confirming hits. So mother started guarding the window herself, standing in the garden with a thin bamboo cane, chasing the birds with cries of 'Haat, haat!' But there would always be a mynah that would return with a hit as soon as she stepped into the house for a glass of water or to take her afternoon nap.

In the end mother resorted to the last option. She started keeping the wooden shutters closed during the day, opening them only in the evenings after sunset. It worked. The nosedives stopped and we started concentrating on buying and selling houses.

Although there are no easy answers for why the birds and the squirrels behaved in such a strange manner, I think it had something to do with the neem trees dying. There seems to be an inverse relationship between the dying of trees and the blossoming of my garden. It was as if some magical panacea had been generously sprinkled on to the ground. The lemon shrub, for instance, started flowering. Fruits started appearing on the chickoo tree for the first time in many years. Even the bonsai pomegranate had little bulbs of red and green hanging from its delicate branches. Something that had never happened before. Mother had a look of disbelief on her face when she tasted her first chickoo from her own garden. 'They are sweet, Robin!' she said with amazement. 'I can't believe they are sweet!'

Only the mogra creeper and the champa tree refused to respond to the panacea. Not once was the champa heavy with the delicate flowers, and numerous attempts to grow a mogra creeper like the one that Dada had carefully nurtured when he was alive failed. 'There is something that Dada did that I don't know,' mother would say once in a while. By contrast there was the champa tree in the neighbour's garden, with its branches drooping over the fence into ours, which seemed to have received the panacea and was blossoming into a resplendent, large bulb of fragrant white.

Maybe it was because of these fruits and flowers that the birds and the animals which had lived spaciously on the neem trees now congregated in our small, congested garden. It seemed to me that not all of our new inhabitants were happy with their new homes. We did not have enough trees to hold such a wide variety of species. The eucalyptus, for instance, barely had room for one crow's nest at the top, and it swayed too wildly in the breeze for a tailorbird to hang its leafy home on one of its branches. The bougainvillea that embraced the barbed wire on top of the garden wall was ideal for the squirrels to play their hide-and-seek games in, but now there seemed to be too many of them for their own comfort. And sparrows would never build a nest in such a thorny network. Of course there were the two wild acacias, the flame of the forest, one wild tree that burst out with incredible yellow flowers during spring, the borsalli tree and the two banyan trees just outside the house, which had branches strong enough to take the weight of any bird. There were the doves (which hated the crows), the green bee-eaters, the kingfishers, the robins, the sunbirds, the rosy pastors, the bulbuls and the crow pheasant. But between them all they did not have enough branches to find a home in.

Perhaps that is why a koel started to coo much before dawn one night, its loud calls ringing unbearably at regular intervals. As a boy I had loved the bird's wavy call. It was the only sound that could abruptly end a game of street cricket. As soon as the bird started calling, the boys would stand under the large neem trees, lean on their bats and stumps, and peer into the leaves to locate the almost invisible, black bird. And then a game of one-upmanship would begin. At first the bird would play along with the boys, keeping a pitch and tempo that could easily be maintained. But soon it would start raising the octave, until the boys would be unable to keep up and start coughing. I remember we would all go home laughing, happy that we had held a conversation with a bird.

Now, in the middle of the night, the same calls were starting to anger me. I wanted to sleep but the bird was too loud. I was hoping the calls would wake up one of the neighbours who would drive it away, so that I would not have to get out of bed. But no one except me seemed bothered. The bird kept calling. Guptanagar kept sleeping. And I could feel anger well up against the bird. The more I tried to shut out the calls by burying my head in the pillow, stuffing my ears with cotton and increasing the speed of the ceiling fan to drown the birdcalls, the angrier I got. In the silent, curfew-struck night, the bird had handpicked me as the audience for its performance. The decibels were being piloted by a deadly accurate kamikaze who avoided an entire city and gunned for my eardrums.

Was the bird playing games with me? On two occasions it fell silent at exactly the same moment as I got up to drive it away. I would put my head on the pillow and allow the thin blanket of sleep to drop gently over me. But the bird would tear into it with a series of shrill calls within seconds of me shutting my eyes. As if it could see me through the walls and the closed doors. When this happened for the third time, I picked up one of mother's broken Kolhapuri chappals and stood in the balcony to identify the tree from where the bird was shooting its decibel arrows. It was the borsalli. The bird called out confidently and I flung the slipper into the direction of the sound with all the force that my rage could summon.

When the slipper hit the tree, I expected one black bird to flutter away and melt into the night.

I was wrong.

A swarm of birds ballooned out in all directions. Thunder. As if reams and reams of paper were being slit with a jagged knife. A thousand clappers were being struck against wooden bells and then thrown upwards into the sky. For a few brief moments, it seemed as if the entire borsalli tree had developed wings and was flying away in fragments. As if the tree was a large koel in flight. There were so many birds in it.

There is only one other instance from my childhood that had made me feel as guilty as I did that night. My sister and I had quarrelled, like siblings do. In a fit of rage I had pushed her. She had stepped on to a piece of broken glass, which had almost severed the little toe on her right foot. The mark from the nasty gash is still there.

Although the bird did not return that night, I slept badly. The silence of the curfew seemed to have magnified the guilt of the borsalli birds. And it hurt more than the call of the koel.

CHAPTER FIFTEEN

Unfortunately, in all this confusion some of the most beautiful birds, the blue jay and the golden oriole, which had till then regularly graced our garden, disappeared. A streak of blue would once in a while fly past in the evening, confirming that the blue jay had found a new home somewhere nearby, but the golden oriole had left forever. The black ibis couple, on the other hand, seemed to have been separated, with only one of them visiting the dry neem tree once in a while. It would sit on the top branches for long hours looking forlorn, and then disappear for days together.

I believe there existed an invisible balance between the trees and the animals in Guptanagar until the neem trees dried up, disturbing the delicate balance forever. Could this have been why the birds and animals behaved in the strange ways that they did? Of course there has to be a scientific explanation for why the mynahs and the squirrels worked in tandem to fill our house with mosquitoes. Or why the koel screeched in the middle of the night. An ornithologist is likely to provide a sound reason, which would probably go against my balance-of-nature theory. But I believe that my explanation holds within it answers to some of the strange things that mother and I would go on to do in the coming days.

I also believe that this wild canopy of bird and animal calls that our garden wove every day until sunset was making it increasingly difficult for mother to move to a new home where there would be no trees and no birds and no squirrels. These sounds were an audible blanket that caressed and cushioned her into believing that there was life around her despite the curfew. It was a blanket that she held on to when she was alone and she was not ready to let go of it so easily.

'How can we live without a garden, Robin?' she once asked me.

'It is better to live without a garden than be dead,' I told her. But she was not convinced. She would go around the city, often without even stepping out of the autorickshaw, afraid that the curfew would be imposed and she would be left stranded outside her house. I fear that more often than not she looked at the trees and the garden than at the house in the hope that her new home would not take away from her the cawing of crows, if not the screeching of the black ibis couple.

Each time after a house hunt, she would come back and talk more about the garden than about the house. 'Nice place,' she said one day after a quick trip in the two hours of curfew relaxation. She had gone out to stock up on vegetables but also popped in to see a house just behind the Vasna bus stand. 'Had all these pillars and a semicircular balcony, but you should have seen the garden. Mogra creepers and all that. Can you believe it? Just like the ones we had in our garden before they dried up. What fragrance . . .'

'How much is it for?' I asked.

'How much is what for?' she asked with a quizzical look,

as if I expected her to know the price of the fragrance of the mogra.

'The house, mother,' I said. 'You went looking for a house, right?'

She looked awkward and took several seconds before answering. 'Eighteen lakhs,' she said slowly as if she was carefully chewing each syllable before spitting it out.

'Are you out of your mind, mom?' I said exasperated. 'Where are we supposed to get eighteen lakhs from?'

'No, no, I know we can't afford it,' she added. 'It is just that the fragrance of the mogra made me nostalgic. That's all.'

'Maybe you can try growing the mogra in our garden for as long as we are still here . . .' I said. 'Considering the sudden fertility in that patch, especially near the acacia, you never know. They may come back.'

'I tried just before the riots,' she said. 'But they never grow. They always burn out.'

'Mom, we have to be looking for a house, not a garden,' I said, realizing that we were looking for safe homes, not gardens.

'Of course, of course,' she said but I could tell she was not convinced. 'But if we can sell the house for eighteen–twenty lakhs then perhaps . . .'

She went to at least one more house with a large garden just behind the Vasna telephone exchange but it was teeming with termites. 'We might have to fumigate it,' she told me. 'It's not a bad place. Large, has a garden . . . Nice champa tree with flowers, not like our champa . . .'

'Mom, we are not looking for a champa tree to live on,' I said sharply. 'We need a house not a tree. And that too a house that we can move into almost immediately so we can get away from all this madness. Not a place that needs to be fumigated . . .'

'Can you be nice to me, Robin?' she said offended. 'Can't I at least tell you when I see something beautiful? Or do we only have to discuss the basics of buying a house . . .'

'But you only tell me about gardens,' I complained. 'Never about the house.'

'What do you want to know,' she said, her voice bristling. 'That it was closed for years, full of dust, crawling with termites? Is that what you want to know? Or should I tell you about the ugly sea-green colour on the walls as well?'

'What are you getting so edgy about?' I said, my voice rising now. 'I am only trying to help. To remain focused.'

'Help? Is this how you help? Then it is better you don't help!'

'What are you shouting about?'

'Am I shouting? Or are you shouting?'

And like so many other mother–son battles our octaves swung like out-of-control pendulums. We fought about everything from not being nice to each other to not understanding each other to many other things that are best not discussed here. What is important is that in the end we tried to resolve the matter by blaming each other's frazzled nerves and the fact that we were cooped up together for such long hours.

Mother's hopes of getting a good price for the house were built around one of the neighbours telling her rather offhandedly that it was easy to get twenty lakh for a house like ours. It had 372 square yards of space, 122 square yards of construction and a pretty garden to boot. Of course there were a few small problems—the house was more than twenty years old, had been damaged in the earthquake, had absolutely no direct sunlight coming into it except in one part of the kitchen in the evening and it sat very close to the 'India–Pakistan border'.

But mother was oblivious to these deficiencies. 'Let all this rioting stop and I'll get it painted from the outside,' she would say. 'And then it won't be so difficult to sell. At least we'll get fifteen lakhs if nothing else . . . Good enough to buy a row house in Satellite, no?'

'Are you sure about all this?' I would ask pessimistically.

'Now don't get my spirits down,' she would hastily add and try to contact a friend of a friend who knew a real-estate broker who was close to a certain well-known builder and was likely to not only help us find a new house but also a prospective buyer for our own house.

But neighbours knew exactly how to get her spirits down. 'Twenty lakhs?' they would smirk. 'Aunty you will not get more than three lakhs for a place like this.'

'Why, what is wrong with my house?' she would ask, offended. She could not believe her home, her only investment in life, was so cheap, so devalued. But she was also aware that the off-white plaster had been peeling off since the earthquake, making the exterior pockmarked. Besides, the cracks that appeared after the earthquake had been filled in with cement but left unpainted, giving the house a badly scarred look. 'I think it just needs to be painted a little,' she would say, making a conscious attempt to hide the uncertainty in her voice, 'and then I can sell it for at least fifteen lakhs, don't you think?'

But many of the neighbours would simply smirk some more and walk away, leaving mother even more confused.

Then a neighbour came with the offer that two shopkeepers from the Guptanagar main road wanted to buy the house for seven lakh rupees, each paying three and a half lakh rupees. This buoyed mother's hopes and she rejected the offer with a firm, 'Nonsense!'

'See? I told you it's worth more than the three lakhs she told me that evening. Let's hold on for just a little more and I am telling you we can sell it for at least twelve lakhs.'

I smiled. 'Mom, you have come down from twenty lakhs to fifteen lakhs to now twelve lakhs. I hope someone is not playing with us . . .'

The confused look was back on her face. But she quickly washed it away and instead lost her patience with me. 'This is what I don't like about you,' she said hurriedly. 'For one, you don't have a solution to all this and then you get my spirits down.' She stomped away to bed and buried herself in a book.

She finally lost hope when she contacted a well-known builder whose father had been Dada's close friend. He told her that our house was effectively on no-man's land. A Hindu would not buy the house at a time like this because it was too close to one of the largest Muslim ghettos in Asia, Juhapura. And a Muslim would not even consider it as he would be in the midst of those who were being seen as the vanguard of the riots. 'Your best hope would be to find a neighbour or someone living nearby, who has money and does not plan on moving out . . .'

Mother was very restless that evening. The sun was starting to dip. The golden light had already begun drawing elongated black shadows on the floor of the house. Dusk. The dried neem trees without their leaves slit the yellow light into larger portions than they had before. Light was bounced off the Formica dining table, reflected on to the glass cabinets and coated everything from mother's snow-white hair to the dull-black wooden chairs with a golden glow.

As usual the rest of the house was immersed in darkness, with pockets of weak afterglow drawing uneven circles on the Freudian couch from the window in the living room.

Mother was starting to feel as if someone had chained her to the dining table with a carefully placed heavy ball of disquiet between her chest and stomach. She was sitting at the table and sipping hot tea as golden as the sunlight. Mother told me later that she felt as if all outlines around her were slowly smudging into one large, golden ball that day. The beer mug with the golden tea was melting into her hand, her golden skin melting into the Formica of the table which was melting into the window even as the mosquito nets were melting into the setting sun. Everything was liquid. Only the large, black ball of disquiet was not melting, holding on to its sharp outlines.

Mother would have loved to rush out of the house, but where could she have gone? There was curfew on the main Guptanagar road and also in many other parts of the old city, where the teeming crowds were her cure against the ball of disquiet. It melted only in crowds.

'But I had to get out,' she told me that evening as I eased into the Freudian couch and switched on the television. She had gone for a long walk in the fields next door and, not surprisingly, talked about trees and more trees. 'Have you seen that tamarind tree just ahead on the left?' she asked. 'It's massive. I have never seen such a huge tree.' She paused for a few brief moments and added, 'In fact everything seemed huge. The neem, the acacia, the peepul, the green almonds . . . Did you know there are marigold fields just beyond the wheat fields?'

I did not.

'They are beautiful. Like a bright-yellow double bed sheet. You should come with me one of these days. We have been living here all these years and haven't even explored our own backyard.'

'You have to thank the curfew for that,' I said.

She ignored the comment and spoke about how the tamarind tree in the fading light reminded her of ghostly tales from her childhood. Most of them, told by her ayah Mani, had witches with twisted feet hanging upside down from the trees, and she laughed eerily, 'I just avoided the tree after that.'

I smiled.

'I mean I know they don't exist,' she said, 'but the last thing I want to do at a time like this is experiment with fear.' She added after a pause, 'What a story that would make . . . Who killed Ester David in the time of the riots? A witch hanging upside down from a tamarind tree!'

We broke out into deep-throated laughter.

'But it is strange that all these trees should seem so huge, no?' she went on. 'Maybe it's the vast open spaces that make them seem so large. Or maybe it is the silence. In fact I think it is the silence . . .'

I can't explain why, but that moment seemed perfect to try and convince her to forget about gardens and trees. 'Do you think we can start looking for a flat, mom, and forget about gardens?' I asked tentatively. 'We can worry about selling the house later. First let's move to a safer place.'

She nodded her head and said, 'Yes, maybe.'

CHAPTER SIXTEEN

Ideally, we should have shifted to a new house in a different part of the city immediately after Geetaben had been stripped and murdered. After all, what better catalyst than bloodshed can you find to hasten a decision related to real estate? Especially when you have a panicky mother and angry mobs looking for men with missing foreskins. The house does not matter. Not whether it has a garden, not what floor it is on, not even the amount of sunlight it receives. The area matters. Any area where you know you are safe despite a curled up, circumcised penis in your underwear. That matters.

But Geetaben's murder was not catalyst enough for mother and me. We were still caught up in little details of gardens and birds, earthquakes and whether Ora would survive in a flat or not. And if we had to invest our meagre financial resources in real estate, it had to be a place we liked. Not a place that made us feel claustrophobic.

I believe that our slow decision-making had something to do with the fact that most newspapers did not carry Sam's photograph of Geetaben's naked body lying in the dust by the side of the road. Had mother seen the photograph, I am certain she would have agreed to live in any pigeonhole away from Guptanagar and away from the riots. She could visualize the dead, naked body in her head, but that image was nothing compared to Sam's photograph.

But then bloodshed can't be your only catalyst in times like these. As mother and I found out, catalysts don't need blood. They need just a little extra fear. In fact three separate incidents that occurred one after another ensured that we moved to a new house within a week. Each represents a higher degree of fear and perhaps explains why we did what we did.

CATALYST ONE: THE BREAKDOWN
Old family friends can sometimes put you in a very awkward situation. They can dig up bits of family history which you would prefer to forget. But for them these bits are jewels of the past that need to be polished and shown off as prized possessions. You have to learn to live with them because the friendship is important.

Yunus Ahmed was one such friend of the family. Among his prized jewels was the story of how he had given Dada company in the days when the rest of us were making one of our failed attempts to settle in Israel. In the process, we had left behind an old man to marinate in his loneliness. Yunusbhai would not hesitate to tell us how Dada had wept like a child on his shoulder, unable to bear the empty house. We would veil our embarrassment and gently change the topic.

Yunusbhai did not mind talking about his own family at times. About how he did not want his two teenage sons to grow up in Juhapura. 'I got the best of both worlds while growing up,' he would tell me once in a while. 'As a Muslim

I have burst crackers on Diwali and flown kites on Uttarayan with Hindu neighbours. And look at my sons now . . . They only get to see one face of our culture. My culture. And I don't like it . . .'

But this was before the riots. Since the riots he was looking for ways of sending his sons to a relative in London. 'I fear for them each time they step out of Juhapura,' he said. 'They can get hurt simply for revealing their true names. I can't live like that.'

That night, a few days after Geetaben's murder, his secondhand Maruti 800 car broke down a little after he had entered the curfew zone. Being a fairly influential businessman in metal scrap, he had managed to acquire a curfew pass. But a little piece of pink paper with the scribbled signature of the additional commissioner of police does not provide any protection when you are surrounded by a mob. Besides, he was a long way from home.

Yunusbhai got off from the car and started pushing it with one hand on the steering wheel. Men came out of their huts in front of the Hajam Mojam ki Dargah and watched him. He must have felt the gaze of hundreds of eyes pinned on him, following his slow movement forward. It is not often that you get to see a middle-aged man push a car singlehandedly on an empty curfew-struck street. A short, cleanshaven man with a handsome face and spectacles, Yunusbhai started to sweat. Not as much from the effort of pushing the car as from fear. In between Anjali Char Rasta and Juhapura, he was defenceless. Normally he would have driven through this stretch at just a little above fifty kilometres, not attracting too much attention by either driving too quickly or too slowly.

Since the riots no Muslim had stopped on the Guptanagar road. The very mention of a Muslim could at times attract a crowd and angry looks. But Yunusbhai had no choice that night. He was walking on an emptied-out road with the weight of a second-hand car tied to his legs, and there was more than two kilometres between him and safety. He had to distract himself from the fear. He started concentrating on the game of umbra and penumbra that the streetlights were playing on the empty tar.

'Need help?' A man approached him with his hands on his waist. His face was partially hidden in the shadows.

Yunusbhai ignored him. 'No, no my home is just here,' he said, pointing vaguely in front of him, not wanting to let the man know that he was from Juhapura.

'Fifty rupees and I will push the car for you,' the man said.

Yunusbhai continued to push the car by himself. 'It's okay,' he said. 'I can manage . . .' Had he allowed the man to push the car, the man would have found out at some point that Yunusbhai was from Juhapura.

But pretty soon Yunusbhai's nearly sixty-year-old back started telling him that it couldn't take the weight of the car any more. His legs started to shiver with the effort.

When a group of policemen finally stopped him to check the curfew pass, he felt relieved. Not because he trusted the police, but because it allowed him to take a breather. The policemen did not offer to help, nor did he ask for it. This was not the time to trust anyone. And he had heard enough stories of policemen leading mobs to not trust the men in uniform.

Help did finally come and from the most unexpected of quarters—a drunk. The thin man wobbled his way to the car, slurred something reassuring and started pushing the car from behind. Yunusbhai did not protest. He was acutely aware that they were in the area where Geetaben had been stripped and murdered, but he tried to banish the thought from his head. He could not afford to panic now. Together they pushed the car for a couple of hundred metres.

Help from the drunk withered away when his wife came running out. If the police saw her man in this state, they would definitely pack him off to jail, she said apologetically and dragged him away, leaving Yunusbhai to himself. Now his throat was starting to turn dry. Every muscle in his body was beginning to ache. There was only one home in the entire locality which he could trust. Our home.

When he finally reached close to our gate, he parked the car by the side of the road and walked up to our door. Mother was shocked to see him at the doorstep. 'Quickly,' he said in between desperate bids to catch his breath. 'Please give me a glass of water before I have a heart attack or something . . .'

Yunusbhai reached his home safely that night and even had the car picked up with the help of a police escort headed by a Muslim police official, but the incident left mother very disturbed. 'He was fighting exhaustion and the fear of dying, and all I wanted was for him to leave. As quickly as possible,' she told me that night when I reached home. 'I feared the house would be attacked if someone found out he was Muslim.' Mother added after a pause, 'I am disgusted with myself.'

What mother did not know was that her fear was not

wholly irrational. At least one person had asked me as soon as I had reached the spot where the car had been parked if it belonged to a Muslim. 'Hai Robinbhai, is this a Muslim car?' a teenage boy had asked, standing in the shadow of a scrap shop.

'How would I know?' I had snapped.

'It is just that the man went to your house after parking the car here and he looked like a Muslim,' the boy added. 'He even went walking towards Juhapura.'

'Don't talk nonsense,' I said and walked off.

I never told mother of this conversation.

CATALYST TWO: CLIPPED BY A BARBER
The air would always be thick with gossip and the fragrance of cheap cologne at Rameshbhai's barbershop on the Guptanagar main road, about five minutes' walking distance from home. This block of white concrete had room for three rickety second-hand barber's chairs with adjustable headrests that never functioned, a cheap, distorted mirror that twisted the reflection at odd places, and a wooden bench with Gujarati newspapers strewn around for customers to kill time while they waited their turn.

But no one buried their heads in newspapers as stories of the neighbourhood would flow as easily as the cups of tea from the tea stall next door. 'Drink, Robinbhai drink,' Rameshbhai would say in between the sound of clipping scissors, and fill me in with stories of how he planned to send his nephew to Dubai to earn extra cash for the family, and how he would soon buy a truck and get into the transport business. Other customers would come in with tales of elopements, wife-bashings, nutty bosses and neighbours' pretty daughters.

Over the years Rameshbhai and I had developed an unspoken bond. He understood how I liked my hair done without me having to tell him. Together we had been through different phases, starting with the Amitabh Bachchan hairdo with the parting in the middle and the sideburns partially covering my ears. Rameshbhai had warned it would not suit my thick, curly mop, but I had refused to listen and he had delivered. Then I saw a photograph a few days later. For the first time in my life I had rushed to Rameshbhai's shop without being taunted about the 'dense forest on my head' and had a neat cropping.

From there I moved to long sideburns, flicks that loosely fell over a small forehead, and finally the ordinary trimming with which I have stayed for the last few years.

About forty days after Geetaben had been murdered, the police relaxed curfew for four hours. I decided to visit Rameshbhai, who had opened the shop after many days. After the haircut and the small talk on how his business had suffered enormously, Rameshbhai got down to giving me a shave, his sharp razor rubbing against my harsh stubble. There was no one in the shop that day. The two of us did not have much to say to each other. There was negligible traffic on the road. The shop was so silent that I could hear the razor brushing against my stubble.

After a while Rameshbhai started the most unexpected conversation. 'So tell me something, Robinbhai,' he said, wiping the foam and the little dots of hair from his razor on to the back of his left hand, 'you are Christian, right?'

He had never asked such a question before. I knew that he had always taken me for a Christian and I had never bothered to explain. 'Why?' I asked a little surprised. 'Why do you ask after all these years?'

Rameshbhai was embarrassed and covered up by saying, 'No I was just wondering... About your caste and all that...'

'I don't have a caste. I have a religion. I am Jewish and we don't have castes,' I said calmly, not wanting to embarrass him any further.

'J... what?' he asked. It was obvious he had never heard the word before.

'Yahudi, Yahudi...' I said, translating it for him.

'Yahudi...' He mulled over the word for a while and then added, 'So are you Christian or not? Not like Muslim, no?'

'Not at all,' I said. I had always found it difficult to explain Judaism to people who did not know that Jews existed among them, but I decided to try all the same. 'We are different. How should I explain this to you... Have you seen that old Bimal Roy film *Yahudi ki Ladki*?'

'No,' he said in a distracted sort of way. 'Don't move your head so much. This razor is sharp. It will hurt and then you will complain I don't know my job...'

'Well then if you haven't seen *Yahudi ki Ladki*... perhaps the best way to explain to you is this. Christians and Muslims broke away from us, the Yahudis,' I said, talking to him through the mirror. 'We were the first and they separated out to go their own way. Muslims were the first to break away and then the Christians separated out. Did you know that Christ lived and died a Jew? Only his followers gave birth to a new religion. I mean it is not as simple as that, but something like that . . .'

'So you are closer to Muslims,' Rameshbhai's remark was the most unexpected after all the explaining. I noticed he was not meeting my eye, concentrating only on my throat.

'Yes . . .' I said hesitantly. 'No . . . I don't know. There are many Jews in the world who don't get along with Muslims, but I can't say I have had problems with them.'

'So it started with you people, all this Muslim thing,' Rameshbhai's tone was starting to change. It was becoming cold and expressionless.

For the first time in so many years I felt as if I needed to take rearguard action after having said something to Rameshbhai. As if I needed to resurrect myself in his eyes. 'Let me explain this to you a little differently,' I said. 'Have you heard of Israel?'

'Yes,' he said but not very convincingly.

'That little piece of land that keeps fighting with its mainly Muslim neighbours?' I asked.

'Not sure. I think I have,' he said, the coldness from his voice refusing to melt.

'That is where we come from,' I said not so confidently. 'Or at least I think that is where we came from 2000 years ago.'

Rameshbhai seemed to have lost interest in the conversation. He quickly wiped my face with a napkin and started putting away his razor.

'Don't you think you should chop off a little more from the top of my head?' I asked. 'I want it shorter.'

Rameshbhai would normally explain in detail the need

for balance in a haircut each time I complained. But now he wanted to keep the conversation as short as possible. 'No, this is good enough,' he said and did not even look up at me.

For the first time I was starting to feel awkward in Rameshbhai's shop. 'Okay then, the usual?' I asked to rekindle some of the warm familiarity I was used to.

'Yes, twenty-five rupees,' he said quietly without looking up from washing his razor.

'Fine, so see you in the next couple of months . . .' I added awkwardly.

'Don't know,' he said. 'Maybe. Maybe not.'

As soon as I left the shop I had a distinct feeling that something old and precious had fallen out of my hands and crashed at my feet. It is difficult to tell exactly what his final remark meant. Was he upset over the fact that the Muslims and I may have shared forefathers a few thousand years ago, or was I reading more into an offhand remark? The doubt still lingers in my head but I haven't returned to Rameshbhai's shop since then.

CATALYST THREE: THE STRANGER
Yunusbhai paid back our friendship and mother's glass of water in the most frightening manner a few days after his car broke down in the curfew zone. 'Estherben, leave Guptanagar immediately,' he told mother on the phone. 'Don't ask me why . . . Just take what you can and get out as fast as you can.'

'Yunusbhai, at least tell me what is wrong . . .' Mother had tried to remain calm. It was early afternoon. I had already left for the office. The streets were starting to thin out after a couple of hours of curfew relaxation. Soon the loudspeakers would start ordering the few people on the streets indoors. Soon the only way to leave home would be the back road through the slums lined up along the fields. The road that we hated to take since Geetaben's murder.

Mother was not keen to leave home like this. She had thought of this moment on a number of occasions in the last couple of months, working out details of what to take and what to leave behind. But when the moment finally came, she froze. Her home, her only refuge she would have to abandon. Where would she go? What would she do?

Yunusbhai did not seem to have the time to answer her questions. 'Estherben, don't waste time, just leave,' he said sounding even more panicky. 'All I can tell you is you are not safe there. There is going to be an attack . . . That's all. It's going to be bad. And please don't tell anyone I called you or I will be in trouble!'

Outside the house, the only place where mother felt safe was with me. She had to reach me. She packed an extra pair of clothes in her runaway bag and rushed out, leaving Ora to the mercy of Leelaben, our maid, who lived next door.

The curfew was yet to be imposed, but no one had waited for the crackling megaphone announcements. There was no one except for a handful of scooterists whizzing past in both directions to reach their end of safety.

The only option was to hitch a ride with one of the scooterists, but this was not the time for scooterists to trust strangers or for mother to trust strangers on scooters. Besides, mother was the last person to hitch her way out of anything. Even in normal times when trust was still alive between strangers, mother would not even dream of sitting behind the scooter of a man she did not know well. Her dignity, mixed with a heavy dose of suspicion, did not allow her to do such things. She would walk half an hour, get dehydrated and sick in the heat and dust, but she would not hitch rides. Rickshaws were safer and allowed her to look stately.

She started taking hurried steps towards the Vasna police station from where she could take one of the by-lanes which had not been shut down by curfew and reach me. Hardly had she walked five minutes when a middle-aged man on a scooter, with a thin moustache and wearing an olive green safari suit, stopped ahead of her. 'Where are you going, aunty?' he asked in Gujarati. 'You know you should not be out like this . . .'

'It's urgent . . .' mother said in a breathless voice. 'Have to get to Ashram Road or I would never have left . . .'

'Okay then, sit,' said the stranger gesturing towards the pillion. 'I will drop you to a rickshaw.'

And mother did. Perhaps for the first time in her life. Only because she thought he was a policeman. 'Thank you,' she said and sat, clutching tightly to her runaway bag. The man did not respond. He just rode quietly.

Mother tried to hold conversation to ease some of the tension in the air and in her chest. She could feel her heart throb through the runaway bag held close to her chest and into the palms of her hands. 'Are you with the police?' she asked as they drove towards Anjali Char Rasta.

'No, the Geological Survey of India,' he said. 'It's a Central government job so I get a curfew pass . . .' His tone was so tense that mother did not ask another question. Besides, it was too late now to get off from the scooter. They rode together, silently.

Once past Anjali Char Rasta, the stranger dropped mother to a rickshaw. 'Thank you very much,' she said. 'You have been a great help. I am Esther David. And you are . . .'

'Please don't ask me my name,' the stranger said politely and disappeared into the increasingly thickening traffic of anonymity where no one could single him out of the mass.

The entire day would go on to be one of the most restless in our lives. Mother reached my office in tears. Friends and colleagues quietened her down with a glass of water and some tea. Frantic phone calls were made to senior police officials to find out about the possibility of an attack and if they could prevent it, but they were certain there would be no attack. They did not even see signs of people gathering either in Juhapura or in Guptanagar.

Mother spent the entire day outside the zone of curfew, reaching home by late evening when it was certain that nothing would happen that day. It was only when she was able to sit down and reflect on the day gone by that she realized her anonymous scooterist was most likely a Muslim. That she had done something extremely dangerous. Had a mob surrounded the scooterist, there was no way that she would have escaped. She collapsed on to the Freudian couch and wept.

'I can't believe someone can be afraid of his own name . . .' mother remarked as we sat down for dinner that night. 'How can you be afraid of your own name?' she asked as she wiped off a tear from her eye.

'I am going to have a word with Yunusbhai,' I said angrily.

He had created more panic. As if we did not have enough of it. 'Really . . . this is how rumours spread and create more trouble.' I would find out much later that Muslims had in fact planned an attack. That it was planned in much the same manner that the residents of Guptanagar had imagined it would be—from across the fields behind my home, and meant to catch us by surprise. If they did not attack, it was because they had no way of circumventing the posse of policemen placed at critical junctures.

Living with this knowledge has not been easy. Had the mob burnt down my house, how would I have responded to Jayendrasinh's remarks about circumcised penises? How would I have responded to Geetaben's murder? How would I have responded to the men who had seen ghosts running in the fields where none existed? I truly don't know. What I do know is that by the end of it all mother and I were ready to move to any house outside Guptanagar, away from bloodshed and stories of possible bloodshed.

CHAPTER SEVENTEEN

The *Times of India*, Ahmedabad reported on the feeling of unease and misgiving among the residents as the rath yatra, the procession of Lord Jagannath, drew near.

> Fears of the possibility of a fresh outbreak of violence were so dominant that people were reluctant to even speak to reporters. The procession would move through some of the most sensitive areas of the city starting from the temple at Jamalpur through Raikhad to Astodia Chakla and Manek Chowk. Some predicted that the streets would be clear of pedestrians—the processionists would be in trucks and the local people would lock themselves inside their homes. In Dal ki Pol and Chor Bazaar, predominantly Muslim, people were planning to move out of their homes, fearing attacks. Shops would remain closed and the police would outnumber the spectators. The MLA from Jamalpur, however, was expected to be part of the ceremony.

∎

'My Six o'clock Syndrome will kill me, Robin,' mother told me as soon as reports of the rath yatra started to appear in the newspapers. 'I can't live cooped up like this any more. Besides, look at all those lucky people in posh areas like Satellite . . . Why should we suffer all this any more? We should get out of Guptanagar before the rath yatra. Violence or no violence, I don't want to live here any more . . .'

Mother's biggest fear was that her past would consume her totally if she was made to confront it every day at dusk. 'I swear I'll go crazy like this,' she told me.

I was afraid that the fights between the two of us would worsen if we were forced to remain locked in any further. That we would become unbearable to each other as time went by. We needed to get out for the sake of sanity.

'Where should I look?' I asked. 'Are you ready for a flat in Satellite or Drive-In or something? Like the Gandhi flat we saw near Manav Mandir . . .'

'Anything will do,' she said. 'Any place where people are not afraid of their own names and rath yatras. Any place.'

'And you will not be able to grow any mogra creepers up there . . .' I said gently, to remove the sting from the comment, but it did not work.

'Let's leave the sarcasm for another day, Robin,' she said, and we started our first concerted effort to find a house without running after illusions like gardens and birdcalls.

Here is a list of flats that we rejected in one day before finding what we thought would be our permanent home outside Guptanagar.

HOUSE NUMBER 1
A two-bedroom flat on the fourth floor off the New Judges Bungalow Road, the latest hip place to be, with newly constructed multistoried shopping complexes coming up

every day. The walls are freshly whitewashed. The windows are large and airy. But none open to the sky, blocked in as they are by the walls of the adjacent towers. Price Rs 5 lakh.

Note: Can be considered. Receives no sunlight.

HOUSE NUMBER 2

A five-minute drive on an inner lane from House Number 1 takes you to House Number 2. Again, a two-bedroom flat with whitewashed walls. But the arrangement of rooms is different. The living room opens directly into the two bedrooms. The balcony opens into the small, pretty garden of the society, but the walls of the bedrooms are blocked in by an ugly red-brick unfinished skyscraper. Builders of the skyscraper have run out of money and are unlikely to complete it for a long time. Price: Rs 5.5 lakh.

Mother's note: Can be considered but one can see straight into the bedrooms as soon as one steps into the house. Robin will have no privacy when he marries.

HOUSE NUMBER 3

At the end of the New Judges Bungalow Road, which connects with the highway leading to Gandhinagar, is House Number 3. No different from House Number 1 except that it is more airy. Price Rs 6 lakh.

Note: Can be considered but seems too far away from civilization. No autorickshaw stands nearby. Mother will have to walk a while just to get a rickshaw, which will make life difficult considering that she is unlikely to hitch rides with strangers any more.

HOUSE NUMBER 4
Bungalow at the end of Drive-In Road, the end that connects to the Gandhinagar highway. A massive place with three bedrooms on the first floor and a large basement which has another two rooms. Has a sliver of a garden between the house and the outer wall lined with henna shrubs, which can be considered as a garden for Ora. Has not been well designed, with cheap wooden fittings everywhere and a flooring of expensive marble—remnants of the owners of the house who have shifted to Mumbai. Price Rs 7.5 lakh.

Note: White plaster is peeling off at many places. Has not been repainted for years and looks rundown. Would need a lot of work to be made liveable. Can be considered despite the price, but do we really need such a large place?

By the end of the day I had seen two more houses, only to be left doubly confused. How do you differentiate between houses, all of which have whitewashed walls, blocked out windows, doodles on the walls and other remnants of past occupants? Ideally, I should have been able to maintain a separate file on each house. After all, mother and I had taken notes and collected brochures wherever possible. But in my head the different characteristics of the houses blended into one large, distorted structure. As if made of wet clay, it would take on a different and abstract form when mother asked questions like, 'Which house do you think has better electrical fittings, House Number 4 or House Number 2?' or 'Do you think we can renovate that last bungalow?'

I would get away by saying, 'Don't know, but you were there too, no . . .'

I was not able to see the six houses as separate structures even when I tried very hard but did not have the courage to tell mother that. After all, we had decided to leave Guptanagar before the rath yatra. The house did not matter, I had told myself again and again. The locality did. A locality in which mother did not have to confront the demons of her past at dusk and I did not have to worry about my missing foreskin.

And yet I did not know what to say when mother asked, 'So what do you think?'

'You want me to make up my mind right now?' I asked.

'What else? I am going with House Number 2. Has a privacy problem, but then you know, it doesn't seem like you are getting married very soon, so . . .'

'Mom, we shouldn't make up our mind like this. I think I need to look at the houses one more time . . .'

'One more time? Come on, Robin, we don't have the time for that. We have seen six houses and now it is time we make up our minds.'

'But, mom . . .'

'No, no, I am tired of all this indecision. First I can't make up my mind and then you can't make up your mind. At this rate we will never leave Guptanagar . . .'

We were all set to start another round of long-drawn-out arguments when a real-estate broker called us to look at one last house that he thought would suit 'people like you'.

'Please . . . not that "people like us" crap again,' I said exasperated. 'How do they decide what "people like us" want?'

'I swear,' said mother, 'as if invisible specifications are written on our foreheads.'

'There is only one thing written on our foreheads. That we are misfits. Maybe we should find other people like us and start a special Misfits Housing Society. That is the only way we will find a house that fits our needs.'

'Do you really know what our needs are?' mother asked.

I did not know what to say.

Mother smirked but we went to see the house all the same. Our doubts were strengthened as soon as we came face to face with the four ten-storey towers standing face to face in two rows.

'What floor?' mother asked.

'Eighth,' the man said.

I looked at him in disbelief.

'I am telling you, you will not have such shock on your face once you see the place.'

Frankly I don't know why we said yes to the house that day. It could have been that we were tired of looking for a house, or it could have been the sheer urgency that the rath yatra and all the other experiences had created. Or it could have been that we truly liked the place. After all, it has the capacity to create a sense of seeming much larger than its 125 square yards. A large sliding-glass door divides the living room from the balcony on the northern side and makes the balcony look like an extension of the living room. The kitchen is divided from the dining area by a short three-foot wall and the windows in the bedrooms again have large sliding glass shutters. Instead of the omnipresent whitewash, the walls are a dull off-white. You can look into the homes of your neighbours in the other towers from the balcony and the bedroom windows, but they are a couple of hundred metres away, to allow for claustrophobia and a respectable amount of natural light. Even today, there are times in the flat when I feel that it is one 125-square-yard room with liquid walls that melt away in my head.

Mother, however, believes that I am romanticizing an ordinary house. 'It is nothing more than a virgin,' she tells me sometimes. 'A brand new house which is neat and clean compared to the rest of the houses, that's all.'

All the same, within a couple of days of the initial visit and after many hours of hesitation on whether we could afford a Rs 7 lakh loan, we found ourselves signing a contract that allowed us to own a brand new flat near Jodhpur Gam. I was acutely aware that this was not too far away from where Jayendrasinh lived in his cocoon of comfort. I had now become part of his cocoon. I no longer had the right to take a higher moral ground of 'understanding the riots better' just because I lived in a riot and curfew zone. I had fled for the sake of sanity. This is something I have never been able to resolve completely. I consider Jayendrasinh's ideas insane, but he lives in that part of the city where I go looking for sanity. We would, however, discover the hard way that sanity and insanity have nothing to do with houses, blocked out windows or the colour of your walls.

CHAPTER EIGHTEEN

Until the riots, the David family had respected a family tradition of never throwing away paper whether it was childhood drawings, love letters, redundant legal documents, books, newspaper articles, diaries, or even unfinished attempts at writing prose and poetry. Until the riots you would have found them scattered all over the house and hidden in the most unexpected corners. On the face of it, the house would not seem besieged with paper, but open the wrong cupboard or touch the wrong pile and you would find yourself being chased by a persistent papyrus monster.

Dada's mounds of cardboard files—in which he maintained everything from love letters to occasional postcards from distant relatives to his first application for a liquor permit in the land of prohibition in 1963—were of course a family legend. Mother too had a few files of letters from people she loved and hated, but she also had gunnysacks full of all the art reviews she had written for newspapers for the past twenty-five years. My sister's main concern was books. For a long time, she would not dispose of the Agatha Christies and other murder mysteries, despite having nothing but disdain left for them, and allowed them to pile up on lofts and glass cupboards in which we could no longer keep new books. And I of course had these Memory Drawers, filled with childhood ink drawings, unintelligible Hebrew dictionaries and dull economics textbooks.

It was not as if we believed we would need these books and letters in the future. We knew they were of no value. Except for a handful of documents, they had no legal importance. Of course many of them had emotional value. In between what now seemed a mountain of inanity there would always be a letter or two that could bring back painful memories. We hoped that if we ignored them, they would disappear from our lives on their own. That was one reason mother ignored Dada's files after encountering them in the initial days of the riots. She had always hoped that the files would one day develop hands and legs, walk out of the house and start lives of their own, away from where she lived. 'I can even leave them something in my will if they don't bicker too much,' she would joke.

Since the riots, especially since buying a new house, we have ended this tradition of protecting the papyrus monster. There was a practical reason behind this decision. Despite its liquid walls, our new house was much too small to accommodate this animal of our memories. Besides, we had decided to make a fresh beginning and try and remove as much clutter from the past as possible. 'I will not let my past burden you,' mother told my sister on the phone.

We created a bonfire in the garden in which, one after another, all the letters and newspaper articles went. Mother was the first to end this long chain of family history by feeding the fire with her art reviews. But we did not dare to create a large fire in which the papers could go in vast quantities.

Smoke billowing from a house in the time of riots gives rise to suspicion. Within minutes you can find yourself surrounded by curious onlookers. Our fire was like an infant who ate slowly but constantly.

It is not surprising therefore that it took us more than a week to dispose of all of Dada's letters. 'Let us just dump all these in the fire without even looking at them,' I had told mother impatiently after reading one of the affectionate exchanges between my estranged biological father and Dada and quickly dropping it into the fire.

'Are you crazy?' mother had said. 'In between all these are important documents of the house. We will need them if we want to sell the house . . .' Seeing that I was becoming restless, mother said, 'Leave all this to me. Go look at your things, especially those drawers. They are a nightmare.'

For the first time since the earthquake, I had to confront the drawers. This time there was no escape.

I emptied the three drawers on to the floor in my room and sat down among notebooks in which I had practised my Hebrew letters, which now looked like garbled messages. There were those love letters from forgotten girlfriends, rusted guitar strings, economics textbooks, knick-knacks I did not even know existed (like the rubber acupressure balls), tonnes of paper that had no value and of course the largest chunk of paper from my childhood—the drawings in black ink of large, dry trees standing naked without their leaves.

A swarm of memories raced through my head—friends and girlfriends, classmates and acquaintances, distant cousins and desperate attempts at strumming a guitar with a hemiplegic hand. There was a specially designed ring with a plectrum stuck to it, which I would fit into my right thumb to strum the guitar by moving my right hand from the elbow. There were even letters from a pen pal I had made much before my last trip to Israel. We had exchanged exactly three letters and then lost interest in each other. Pinned to one of her letters was her photograph, obviously taken with a cheap camera. Sitting in open fields in shorts, she looked pretty.

As I rummaged through this pile of memories, my hand fell on an old piece of folded white paper. In the more than ten years that it had lain inside this drawer, it had turned slightly pale and brittle. I could not see its contents as it was folded inwards. But I knew what it was. It was my first attempt to write my own mourner's Kaddish on the day Dada died.

I opened it gingerly, not wanting to tear it at the folds. My handwriting seemed less shaky then but just as messy. It seemed to hold a faint scent of catsnip leaves, the kind that are used at the graveyard on the seventh day after a person's death.

The scent reminded me of my dislike of the rituals for the dead. The way they bathe the naked body in an old and dented aluminium bathtub kept in the synagogue, the way they dress the body in freshly ironed clothes for the last time, buy fresh cotton cloth to stitch a sacklike shroud, sprinkle Jerusalem sand on the closed eyelids, and the way the entire congregation chants the Kaddish, punctuating it with 'Amens' at precise points without understanding a word of Hebrew, it all seems to point to one thing—Disposal. The movie of your life has reached its final frame. The End.

There is one other aspect about the rituals that stinks of

finality. Sometimes, while washing the dead body, the bathers crack jokes about the size of the genitals of the corpse. You crack jokes about a person's genitals in his presence only when you are dead certain that he is not going to jump up suddenly and scream, 'Madarchod!'

I remember well the day my grandfather died. I had stood too close to his face for my mother's comfort. 'Aye!' she had said gently tapping me on my right shoulder. 'What are you doing? Stop staring at him like that. He is dead. Cry a little if you want. You'll feel better.'

'I don't feel like crying,' I had said.

'Arre, cry baba. I'm telling you'll feel better,' she had almost implored with affection, assuming I was in a state of shock. 'Everybody cries.'

But I had not felt like crying. Maybe because I could not believe that Dada's brain, which had for nearly eighty years conjured up jokes about spiky garden lizards running up the assholes of schoolteachers, which had documented and bred rare albino animals and birds, and which had painstakingly created a scrapbook of the most gruesome of human crimes from around the world and named it *I Shall Fight Darwin*, had turned into nothing more than a rubbery lump of flesh. My doubt had been strengthened by his wrinkled and shrivelled-up face, which had an expression that can best be described as a smile. And if he was smiling, he could not be dead.

Dr Dinesh Devani, our family doctor, had held Dada's wrist gently to check his pulse, run his stethoscope up and down the cold chest, pursed his lips and shaken his head as if trying to draw an 'eight' with it. That was his way of certifying

Dada dead without having to say the word 'dead', and we had understood. But a bizarre thought crept into my head and refused to go away. What if Dada was not dead? What if Dr Devani had made a mistake? Was it possible that Dada had taken a joke too far? He was, after all, smiling. It was not difficult to see him struggling to break free from the shroud under mounds of heavy mud with the Jerusalem sand irritating his eyes, even as the mourners slowly started to move towards the dirty roadside tea stall next to the graveyard for their routine snacks after each burial. I could not bear the thought of Dada suffocating and not dying, agonizing forever, unable to reach up to his eyes and remove the golden sand.

By standing close to his face, I was trying to confirm that he was dead. The problem was the closer I got, the more uncertain I became. I thought I saw the upper lip twitch one time, and something glimmer in his half-closed eyes for the briefest of moments another time. It was the kind of flickering you see when you are alone in the house and catch in the corner of your eye a silhouette, a shadow, the end of a sari pallu, something, moving from one room to another. You know you are alone and what you have seen is nothing more than your brain playing tricks. And yet, there are times when you get up and check. Just to be sure.

It was that sort of final check that I was making before the battalion of industrious Bene Israel women settled in the house with their ancient hand-operated sewing machine to stitch together the shroud. I had this distinct feeling that something was trying to jump out of Dada's body to tell me that he was only joking and that he was in fact alive, but a powerful force at the base of his stomach was pulling it back.

Perhaps I would detect something in the little hole in the middle of his throat.

A speck of dust. That was his breathing apparatus. Smoking one carton of Panama cigarettes a day had led to cancer of the larynx. His lungs had been disconnected from his nose and attached to this hole. I had taken one more step and was so close to his face that his upturned, thick, white moustache was starting to tickle my cheeks. The hole had shrunk in the last twenty years, so it needed some effort. Our noses were about to rub when mother had interrupted with her gentle 'Aye' and tap on the shoulder.

A lot changed when Dada died. For instance, I was to suddenly become the most important person in the family at least for that one day. Because of Dada's death, because mother had divorced her husband even before I had learnt to walk, because she did not have a brother and because my elder sister could not become a man, the yoke of being the eldest male member of the family had fallen on me. I was to stand over Dada's head with a candle in hand and recite the mourner's Kaddish.

And because I had never made an effort to memorize a single Hebrew prayer, I had no choice but to repeat the Kaddish after Mazgaokar Uncle, a thin, stern-looking elder of the community, who never showed unnecessary emotion and asked only necessary questions like, 'Do we have a minyan?' or 'Have you brought the Jerusalem *chi mati*?' No one needed to tell him that I did not know my prayers. Having seen me in the synagogue only on Yom Kippur day, he had already broken down the Kaddish into small morsels for me to swallow. '*Yisgaddal Ve'Yiskadash Sh'may Raba . . .*' he had said, looking at me from over the low-lying spectacles on the rim of his nose with raised eyebrows and a wrinkled forehead, as if inquiring if I was up to it. But I had withstood the pressure. '*Yisgaddal Ve'Yiskadash Sh'may Raba,*' I had repeated, without quavering to restore some confidence in Mazgaokar Uncle. '*B'alma Dee'vra Hisrusay,*' he went on, but this time the inquiring look was gone, and I started to relax just a little. '*B'alma Dee'vra hi . . .*' I was starting to lose it. '*Hisrusay,*' Mazgaokar Uncle came to my aid with the inquiring look back in place.

Meaningless Hebrew words were starting to turn into little torn pieces of paper and floating downwards into a dark abyss that had opened in front of me. I was expected to catch them before they glided away out of reach. I could feel the judging eyes of the hundred Jews who, I thought, held back from smirking at my ignorance only out of respect for the dead body. Unfortunately I did not catch all of what was thrown at me. Some of the Hebrew smithereens did disappear into the abyss.

After that, the only part of the ceremony I focused on was letting the melting wax from the candle trickle on to my fingers. The molten liquid would singe for a few moments and then thicken to become part of my skin, a boil that had no sensation. I felt almost sensuous pleasure in peeling it off. As if I was peeling off my own skin without pain. The only thought that danced in my head in between the peelings and the occasional 'Amens' was to find out what exactly those Hebrew words, which had stammered out of my mouth, meant. Why did they sound so hollow? As if someone else had said them and I was a mere spectator to the entire exercise? I had to find out.

After burying Dada in the six-and-a-half-foot rectangular hole next to my grandmother's grave in the increasingly crowded graveyard, and flinging the catsnip leaves at the entrance with my back turned to his mound of dust, I went to the only prayer book there was in the house with an English translation and thumbed out the Kaddish.

'Glorified and sanctified be God's great name throughout the world which He has created according to His will.' That was okay. After all it was a prayer, and by definition it had to accept that we were on this earth because He wanted us, or did not want us, to be here.

'May He establish His kingdom in your lifetime and during your days, and within the life of the entire House of Israel, speedily and soon; and say, Amen.

'May His great name be blessed forever and to all eternity.' How many times did we have to accept that He was the boss? There was more.

> Blessed and praised, glorified and exalted, extolled and honoured, adored and lauded be the name of the Holy One, blessed be He, beyond all the blessings and hymns, praises and consolations that are ever spoken in the world; and say, Amen.

> May there be abundant peace from heaven, and life, for us and for all Israel; and say, Amen.

> He who creates peace in His celestial heights, may He create peace for us and for all Israel; and say, Amen.

Did the mourner's Kaddish at no point refer to the dead and how much we would miss them? Did God fear that all those who had to face the death of a loved one would abhor him? That he would be held responsible for grief and in the process be rejected by mankind as the Supreme Being?

That night I had created my own mourner's Kaddish. I had promised myself that if I ever stood over the head of a dead body and prayed again, this is what I would say, and this is what that sheet of paper contained:

Dear loved one,

All of us who have gathered here today accept that we don't completely understand the flame of life and how it is extinguished. In fact we don't even know if life is a flame that can be extinguished, or if there is a different dimension to being dead. What we do know is that we loved you with all our hearts through the good times and the bad, through the moments of affection and wild rages of hate. We loved you and that is what we will remember as you live on in our memory.

The words had seemed thoroughly childish then and they seemed thoroughly childish now. I remembered I had told myself then that I would write another Kaddish Dada would have been proud of, folded the paper, put it in the drawer and left the task for another day.

And then I had forgotten about it. For thirteen years it gathered dust until the time came for us to leave Guptanagar. I was faced with my promise. I then realized that a Kaddish should be an extremely personal affair, a new one for each dead person you cared enough for. So in the midst of the rubble of my past I finally wrote these lines as my final Kaddish for Dada:

> When the needle of time pointed at you, you did go silently.
> You of the larynxless electric voice who spun folk tales
> Of spiky garden lizards climbing up anuses of stern schoolteachers
> And paraded emu eggs as that of buffaloes.
>
> You of the upturned moustache
> Who lived among singing canaries
> And stuffed king cobras
> And the madness of African bees trapped in a glass jar, dead.
>
> You of the guzzler fame
> Who drank more rum than ruffians
> And wept voicelessly with cranky ghazals
> And sang with the chimes of wall clocks synchronized to a cacophony.
>
> You of the striped pyjamas
> Who was swallowed by loneliness
> And demanded your dead body be bathed in the ittar of roses
> And that your shroud carry your wife's letters in ashes in a plastic bag.
>
> You of the fighter of dust
> With peacock feather dusters

Who did go silently
Twelve years before the earth trembled
Thirteen years before blood stained your doorstep.

Or did you?

That night the curfew was totally lifted from the Guptanagar main road.

CHAPTER NINETEEN

Had I not included the wall clocks in the personalized Kaddish for Dada, it would have been incomplete. He was obsessed with their incessant ticking in the living room. A garishly painted cuckoo clock, a tall, stately grandfather's clock decorated in Chinese lacquer, an elegant Seth Thomas with weathered, dark-brown wood and an antique musical clock, all were synchronized to such perfection that they chimed every half hour at almost the same time. Dada was obsessed with winding them up every morning and ensuring that they tick away for the rest of the day. The ticking even controlled his moods. If a clock malfunctioned he would become irritable and snap at everyone. He would call in almost every watchmaker in town and fret and fume until it started ticking again.

Dada had also developed an ear for the synchronized chiming of his favourite clocks. If one of them did not go off with the rest, he would leave a conversation, however important, midway and spend the next few minutes adjusting the arms and checking the swing of the pendulum.

It was not surprising therefore that in his entire life Dada had never missed an appointment or reached a function late. To catch a train, he would reach the Kalupur railway junction ninety minutes before time and expect the rest of the family to be there with him.

Why he was so obsessed with time and ticking clocks I could never tell, but I believe his fear of dying and his inability to come to terms with his loneliness had something to do with it. He was not the kind of person who would openly admit to his fears. If a conversation veered towards the topic of death, he would say, 'When the needle of fate points at me, I will go silently.' Of course family and friends would then gather around him and say, 'Who, you Dada? You are strong enough to twist any needle. Just like in the bodybuilding days of your youth.' He would enjoy the attention, sit back twitching his upturned moustache and smile. As long as the clocks were ticking, he felt he had time left.

Mother and I, however, had no time left. We had decided to move before the rath yatra and, considering the number of objects we had to deal with, there was no time. We had to categorize each object and decide whether we wanted to keep it or discard it. And if we wanted to keep it, did we have place in the new house? The clocks, as we would later regret, made it to the list of objects we would have liked to keep but did not have space for. Besides, mother claimed she was tired of promiscuous geckos, overzealous spiders and dust crawling in and out from behind the clocks. We gave away the musical clock to a family friend as a gift and sold the grandfather's clock and the cuckoo clock to an antique dealer for next to nothing. The Seth Thomas we kept for my sister, who had told mother she would one day take it to her house in France.

'Our new house is not going to be a playground for mating geckos. And look at all the dust that collects on them,' mother had said after giving them away. She was not completely wrong. Before the first monsoon clouds gathered over Ahmedabad, the geckos would turn our living room into a garden of lovemaking, chasing each other's tails, frolicking and mating, completely oblivious to our presence.

We used this excuse to get rid of a lot of things from the house during that time. Many of them were truly beautiful objects, which we should never have given away. Like the two large, black Egyptian pickle jars in the garden in which Dada used to grow bonsai pomegranate, or the temple stone carving of weather-beaten, faceless dancers and drum players that Dada claimed were more than 400 years old, or the sensuous Chinese and Japanese vases on which delicate dragons breathed fire, or the empty Chakor cages intricately woven out of wire mesh, so small that it was difficult to believe there was a bird small enough to fit into it. Or even the musical cigarette lighters and the antique ashtrays that Dada had carefully collected over the years.

There were also the carved capital seats, which needed a heavy dose of Gamaxine powder to remove the labyrinthine colonies of ants in them, or some of the brass artefacts that we gave away without stopping to think if we were doing the right thing. There was a Persian carpet rolled up in Dada's cupboard. There was some blue Jaipur pottery and many other objects, all of which we now talk about in the past tense.

It was as if the riots had set into motion a terrible churning, a manthan of the samudra of objects in our house. Fear was the stick, and the smallness of our new house the rope with which this churning was taking place. Everything was turning, revolving, floating, leaving the house. The nectar of life, we thought, would come from shifting to the new house where there would be no fear. Where there would be no men who were afraid of their names. Where there would be no men looking for other men with circumcised penises to kill. Where there would be no naked corpses lying a stone's throw away from what we would call home.

But before that, before we could drink the nectar of life, this manthan, this churning, had to be completed. And so we gave. Without thinking, without regretting. Nothing seemed more important than that pot of the nectar of life. It was a thick whirlpool of numerous objects turning, spinning, disappearing. We had been caught in the churning, pinned to its invisible walls, hoping to break free.

There are times when I think it was a good thing we panicked and gave many of the possessions which we had no room for but clung on to because they were either beautiful or because we felt a strange guilt for abandoning what Dada loved. But there are other times when I feel that utility can't be the only reason for holding on to objects from your past. Had we not panicked, we would perhaps have made our house beautiful and more liveable with them. Or at least some of them.

There was another reason too why we got caught in the whirlpool of giving away. It had something to do with Dada's inability to throw away anything. In his nearly eighty years, he had collected everything from the totally mundane to the unbelievably exotic, and always found corners in the house to store them or display them proudly. Over time, the walls were covered with everything from the busts of growling lions as trophies from his hunting days to tonnes of photographs of him standing next to celebrities.

In fact the living room was a museum of his eccentricities. Starting with the stuffed king cobra standing erect with its thin hood in a glass box. Its marble eyes followed you everywhere in the room and could be very unnerving for people suffering from ophidiophobia or fear of snakes. Like mother, who could not ignore the serpent sitting still in the corner of her eye. Sometimes she would cover the glass case with a piece of cloth to be able to concentrate on the conversation with a guest. Next to it, without a glass box, sat a coiled puff adder, its large, diamond-shaped head resting on its curled-up back. There was also the bust of a spotted deer, two snouts with spikes of swordfishes fashioned into swords, and a small beaker full of African bees. Add to these the stuffed finches and canaries placed carefully among a large collection of antique betel-nut cutters, a paan box shaped like a car, chinaware, emu eggs, a Dilruba packed in a plastic case and an old but powerful air rifle used to keep the langurs at bay from Dada's precious garden.

But this collection was nothing compared to the slim metal rack he kept near the entrance to the house. On the top shelf, in a large, glass beaker filled with formalin, he kept a human foetus with two heads. Many years ago, Dada had bought it from a travelling mini circus where it was displayed as a freak of nature. It was a grotesque sight, this stillborn child sitting on its haunches in a glass box filled with a thick liquid, its wrinkled skin having turned a pale white over the years, the right hand resting on the knee and both heads tilting slightly to the right.

The rest of the beakers were less exotic but only in comparison to the two-headed monster. There was a two-month-old lion foetus, a hyena foetus, a panther foetus and the foetus of a great grey kangaroo. There were also scorpions, sidewinders, trinket snakes and a goat kid born with eyes under its palate that lived for twenty-four hours.

Removing this rack from the house was one of the smartest things mother could have done immediately after Dada's death. I shudder to think of what would have happened if we had not rid ourselves of it before the earthquake struck. Most of the beakers would have crashed, leaving us with the job of cleaning the floor of the rotting foetuses lying in a soup of stinking formalin and broken glass.

Dada's eccentricity also led him to challenge animal-related superstition. Here is a press note he released in the local newspapers and later put up as one of his proud displays in the living room as a plaque:

> Avail of a golden opportunity to win Rs 5,000 if, of course, you can survive to collect the amount. The honorary advisor, Hill Garden, Zoo, Ahmedabad Mr Rueben David has announced an award of Rs 5,000 to anyone who can cure a bite from a venomous snake by magic, mantras, black stones, Naagmani, herbs, or by virtue of any other means other than anti-snake venom serum. One condition imposed by Mr David is that the venomous snake, which would be induced to administer the bite to the person, will only be provided from his collection.

> More than a year has elapsed since Mr David made this offer but no one has plucked the courage to accept it. The so-called healers succeed in curing only non-venomous snakebites. Many innocent victims of poisonous snakebites have lost their lives because of these wicked, self-styled healers, but where are those healers now? Why don't they come forward and accept this lucrative offer? Mr David is certain that no one will come forward to accept this offer.

The press note, released on 1 September 1982, went on to say that he made this offer from the standpoint of humanity and not because he was rich.

There were other placards as well. Like this quote from George Bernard Shaw: 'When man hunts animal, he calls it sport. When animal hunts man, he calls it ferocity.'

The one that startles me even today is this one: 'I strongly believe that we are outgrowing the balance of nature, and in time to come we will be left to eat one another, leaving the animals and birds aside.'

Amidst all this lay two of Dada's proudest possessions. There was the framed picture of his youth from the time he was a bodybuilder. The sepia-tainted picture shows his torso in soft glow, with his muscular arms folded in front of his chest making him look handsome and confident. Beside it was the framed Padma Shree scroll that he received in 1975 from President Fakhruddin Ali Ahmed in the presence of Prime Minister Indira Gandhi for creating the Ahmedabad zoo and conducting unusual experiments in it. Like making it the first zoo in the world to breed flamingos in captivity.

Or having one of the rarest collections of albino animals, including an albino porcupine and a crow.

Except these two frames, mother had given away much of the exotica to schools and colleges and to the Rueben David Natural History Museum, a museum of stuffed animals carefully placed in artificially created natural habitats of the animals.

Many of Dada's friends even castigated us for removing these objects from the house. As if we were ridding ourselves of Dada's memory along with the objects soon after his death. 'It seems as if you were just waiting for Dada to die,' one of them told mother with a wry smile. But then he did not have to live among spider webs and breeding geckos. And he was not going to clear away the mounds of dust for us, like Dada used to. Besides, who would explain to him that when Dada was alive, mother, Amrita and I had been pushed into a small part of the house? Except for one almirah and three beds, we owned nothing in the house. At least after his death we could hope to make a little room for ourselves, perhaps hang a picture on the wall that we loved and did not belong to Dada and the past.

The barbs had, however, affected mother. After sending the rack to the museum and the snakes and other stuffed animals and birds to the biology laboratory of a college, she had slowed down the process of giving away things to avoid the biting sarcasm. She locked away many of the objects in cupboards and stacked them away in the mezzanine. Those objects that did not fit in the cupboards or the mezzanine were allowed to remain in their original places, until one of the objects from the cupboards was discreetly given away.

Now, with the date of the rath yatra approaching, shielding ourselves from barbs of Dada's friends seemed a luxury. Besides, Dada's memory had faded from the minds of his friends as well. According to them it was now justified to give his collection, to the extent that some even approached mother with requests. 'I am really interested in the brass artefacts, Estherben,' they would call up and say. 'Please think of me if you are giving them away.' Or even, 'Those Chakor cages, Estherben? Do you intend to keep them?'

Without reminding any of them of their barbs, mother gave away what she could. 'At least they will take care of it,' she told me after giving some of the delicate chinaware. Once in a while she would look at the odd, beautiful object and ask, 'Do you think this would fit into the new house?' Depending on my response, mother would make up her mind on whether to keep it or not. And we kept very little, like books, a little furniture including the Freudian couch and the Formica dining table on which the evening sun used to glow, some brass artefacts that mother loved and the antique multicoloured glass lanterns that Dada used to switch on only once in a while.

Slowly, as the house started to empty out, my voice started to echo on the bare walls. The glass cabinets in the living room started to throw my reflection back at me.

Packed to the brim with objects of the past, echoes and reflections had never lived in our house before. The glass cabinets always had objects painted in a million colours, the camouflaged reflections never allowing them to glide past without first diffusing them. The walls, on the other hand, were covered with framed photographs and hunting trophies from Dada's youth, which did not allow sound to ricochet. But now the reflections started to follow me, chase me, often taking the forms of friends and family members who did not live around us any more, but had been an important part of me in the past. Is that Amit, my tall, gangly college friend resembling my reflection? In December 1992 he had casually come home for an afternoon of gossiping and talking about movies that he one day hoped to direct. The Babri Masjid had been demolished just the day before and violent riots had broken out all over the country that morning.

That was the first time curfew had been clamped on Guptanagar, and Amit had been stuck in my house for ten days. Although he was most comfortable, his biggest grievance was the western style toilet. More used to the Indian style, he had complained, 'How do you guys manage without the pressure of the squat?' It left him constipated for three days until he discovered his own ingenuous way to bring pressure to bear on his bowels. He taught himself to delicately balance in the squatting position on the rim of the western commode. And once he had perfected the balancing act, he would come out of the toilet smiling. Something the two of us joke about even today.

Is that Tejal walking along my reflection in the glass cabinet? Her smooth, brown skin, her telling eyes and a mouth that was a slightly smaller version of Angelina Jolie's had turned me into her obedient dog on a leash. But she would never let me lay a hand on her. We would sit for hours on the Freudian couch talking, with me ogling her glistening chest with the tip of her cleavage peeping out from her loosely buttoned shirt. She is one of the few women I am still in love with. But she is too far away, practising medicine on the beaches of New Zealand.

There were of course other women who had come and gone from my life, but somehow in the last few days in Guptanagar, it was only Tejal who kept appearing and disappearing from between reflections.

There were other reflections—my sister joking, laughing, fighting with me on the dining table. Telling me stories of an unimaginable underworld throbbing with magical characters right under our feet, of which she was a member, and how, one day when I grew up, she would make me a member too. I believed those stories and she enjoyed the awe on my face.

Is that Dada with his elder brother, Dr Jacob David, sitting in the living room, sipping black rum and talking of times gone by? Is that Manali with her unbearable guilt of having exposed her large breasts to me? Is that my guitar teacher strumming Don Williams and Billy Joel? Is that me in the reflection, or is it all of them?

There were times when I felt that there was more than one person between mother and me as my voice bounced around in echoes. As if another person was speaking on my behalf without my permission. At other times the same echoes and reflections made me feel hollow and lonely. The empty space would seem emptier. For the first time, I was small in comparison to the house, and growing smaller all the time.

It was only on the last day in the house that I realized what made Dada never throw away anything and why he was so obsessed with the ticking of the wall clocks. As I stood alone in the empty living room one last time for a brief moment, I realized that Dada too must have felt hollow and small and lonely in large, empty houses. Like mother and me, he too must have seen memories of people in the echoes and the reflections. Like mother, who found solace in rubbing shoulders with strangers in crowded streets at dusk to beat her Six o'clock Syndrome, he too hoped to chase away the echoes by filling the house with as many objects as he could.

I started to realize then that I had felt something he must have felt. That I was no different from him. He was I and I he. The one exception was that he had found a way of fighting the echoing ghosts. I had not.

CHAPTER TWENTY

The picture is telling. It is an old black-and-white family portrait of a husband and wife and their four young children. The three daughters are standing together like a stiff clot on the right side of the frame. Behind them stands the thin father, wearing what looks like a cheap suit. Next to the girls sits the frumpy mother in a pale-coloured sari with the only son, who seems like the youngest child of the family, sitting on her lap. The photograph tilts slightly to the right, hanging gingerly by a thin wire on a wall so badly cracked that it is a miracle it is still standing.

Another photograph shows a middle-aged woman, her saffron sari covering her head, laughing with her mouth wide open. Her uneven teeth sparkle as a warm evening sun washes her face. Her wrinkles look stretched in the process.

Mother was standing in the middle of the living room of our new home holding a yellowing copy of a newspaper in her hands. I had caught the pictures on the newspaper from the corner of my eye. I could tell that I had seen them somewhere but it was difficult to place them. To tell which part of my past they occupied. And leafing through my memory was difficult in between the maelstrom that the movers and packers had unleashed.

Mother had just written a cheque out to the movers and packers. She had ensured that most of the objects needed immediately were in the right places. The dining table had been set just outside the kitchen. Mother's bed had been moved into the inner bedroom. The Freudian couch had been placed by the southern wall in the living room. Even the kitchen had been set, the gas stove attached to the cylinder, the glassware unpacked and set on the shelves. Lilaben, our old maid from Guptanagar, was making some hot tea with milk and mint for our first cup of the evening in our new home. It was an important act, drinking mint tea in the new house. It would mean final confirmation that we had shifted.

The three Godrej almirahs were the only things which created trouble. They were too large to be manoeuvred into mother's bedroom and now occupied my much smaller bedroom, taking up the space that I was hoping to leave empty. 'My fate is tied to them,' I told mother, as the memory of the ungainly almirahs turning into supple belly dancers just the year before crossed my mind. Such liquid grace these ugly giants had shown then, dancing with the earthquake. But these were not thoughts you share with a panicky mother on your first day on the eighth floor. The memory of the earthquake had to be kept out. The problem was that earthquakes have a mind of their own.

We had just closed the door and locked ourselves in our new home for the first time when mother asked, 'Robin, what is this doing here?' She had a strange look on her face. As if a dead man had walked past her and she could not decide whether it was a crude joke or an apparition. She thrust the old newspaper towards me.

It was a copy of the *Times of India* of 6 February 2001, barely ten days after the earthquake had struck. The two photographs had been placed around the lead story. The caption for the first one read: 'An old family photograph is all that remains of this house at Ramaniya village in Mundra Taluka of Kutch'. The second caption read: 'Jellu laughs while receiving counselling for post-traumatic stress disorder from a CARE official at Kotdi village'. 'Skeletons Begin Tumbling out of Builders' Cupboards' read the lead headline. The straps read, 'Swift debris clearance may help errant developers go scot-free' and 'PIL for inclusion of "quake code" in norms'. The main story talked about a cruel irony. The municipal officials had to remove the debris to ensure that there was no one still trapped under it. Also, stinking dead bodies could not be allowed to remain buried under these earthquake-made tombs. But if the debris was removed, the police would lose evidence needed to frame charges against builders who had allegedly used poor material in the collapsed buildings. The anchor piece talked of the former ruler of Kutch who claimed to be a direct descendant of Lord Krishna and was living in a tent, as his palace had collapsed. Who were we to complain when descendants of the gods had not been spared, I remembered joking with colleagues.

I also remembered taking responsibility for the photo-feature on the back page that day. The lead picture was a sad and frightened woman walking out of her flat with pillows in her hands. Behind her a man Friday carried folding chairs and a carom board. She was leaving home for the sake of safety. She was running away from the earthquake.

What could have been more ironical? We were in the same

position as this woman. In one year, only the nature of the disaster had changed. I had unknowingly scripted my own future in some odd way on 6 February 2001.

'Where did this come from?' I asked.

'No idea,' mother said. It was obvious from her voice that she was not pleased by the sight of an earthquake edition.

'It has to have come from somewhere,' I said getting even more puzzled.

Mother looked at me, standing in the middle of the room with her hands on her hips.

'Mom, where did you find this?' I asked a little irritated by both my mother's lost look and the discovery of the newspaper.

She did not say anything and pointed to the table next to her in the living room.

The discovery of an old newspaper should not have been such a big issue. But mother had become extremely sensitive to words like 'tremor' and 'earthquake' ever since we had shifted to the eighth floor. The mere mention of the words would make mother cup her ears and screech, 'No, no, no, I don't want to hear those words! Please shut up . . .' The words were like keys that opened doors to her fear of her house collapsing on her. She believed that if she did not hear the words those doors would never open.

The next few minutes were spent trying to trace the origins of the newspaper. Likely sources were looked at.

'Do you think the builder left it there to tell us that his flats are quake-proof?' mother asked.

'Sounds ridiculous,' I said, but went through each and every page in the hope of finding a piece which would glorify our builder all the same.

When the attempt failed, we called up the movers and packers hoping that perhaps they could tell us something, a clue that would help us unlock this mystery. Their reply was curt. 'We don't keep track of old newspapers,' they said. 'Besides, we did our packing in the old house. There was no need for us to bring along waste . . .'

'Someone is playing a prank . . .' mother finally said. 'Has to be a prank . . . Someone is trying to purposely disturb me . . .'

'Mom, who would have the time and energy to work out such an elaborate prank?' I had no strength left for conspiracy theories. 'Whoever it was would have had to know beforehand that we were moving to the eighth floor, someone who knew you can't hear the "E" word, someone who made the extra effort to dig out an old newspaper and then place it here without being noticed in the new house. Has to be very motivated to think up such mind games. Or maybe someone is paying him to play mind games with us . . .'

Mother did not retort like she normally does and I decided to play down the issue before it spiralled out of hand. I did not want to start a new life in a new home with a fight, and neither did mother. If we wanted to test the thinness of the walls and how far our voices would travel if we screamed, we could do it another time. 'Must be nothing, mother,' I said in an offhand manner. 'It must have been lying somewhere hidden in the house and the packers must have picked it up unconsciously with the rest of the stuff . . . Must be nothing . . .'

But mother was not convinced. She dug into the many

cardboard boxes left unpacked, pulled out an old steel mezuzah complete with a small glass window from which the Hebrew letter 'shin' was visible, made extra efforts to find a carpenter and had it nailed to the entrance of our flat.

'Why don't we sacrifice a goat and smear the door with its blood? That should give us divine protection against conspiracies and curses . . .' I wanted to tell mother. But like two experienced, competing dancers, we knew each other's moves perfectly. So I knew how she would have responded. 'Don't underestimate the power of the mezuzah,' she would have said sharply. 'Don't forget nothing happened to our house either in the earthquake or in the riot. Isn't it possible that this piece of steel protected us? That is what it is supposed to do, right? Protect us from disaster?'

'In that case we should never have left Guptanagar . . .' I would have said and started another elaborate round of arguments, which in turn would only have strengthened her doubts. So I said nothing.

The aim was to help mother settle down, to relax a little and then complete the rituals. So I shut up, hoping that, if nothing else, the mezuzah would settle the whirlwind rising in her chest.

Neighbours had gathered around while the mezuzah was being nailed. They had asked its significance. 'Just a ritual . . .' mother had said with a shrug of the shoulders, not wanting to get into the story of the ten plagues and the killing of the firstborns of the Egyptians. That is not how you start a conversation with neighbours when you meet them for the first time. That this little piece of steel was linked to a story dating back to a time when the firstborns of an entire nation had to die, so that we, the Jewish people, could be freed from slavery. 'Just as you paint a swastika on your entrance and install a Ganesha in a new home for auspicious beginnings, we put this little thing . . .' she told one of the neighbours.

'Do you know the blessing for nailing a mezuzah?' mother asked after it had been nailed. She knew well that in our family, we knew only one blessing well. That of lighting the Shabbat candles which goes like this:

Baruch Atah Adonai Eloheinu Melech Haolam
Asher Kidehenu Bemitzvasov Vetzivanu
Lehadlik Ner Shel Shabbat Kodesh.

It translates into:

Blessed are You, Lord our God, King of the universe,
who has sanctified us with His commandments,
and commanded us to kindle the light of the holy
Shabbat.

So we improvised.

Blessed are You, Lord our God, King of the universe,
who has sanctified us with His commandments,
and commanded us to nail a mezuzah on the entrance
of our homes.

Mother put a hand on my head and said, 'Welcome to your new home . . .'

'It is your home too, mother,' I said.

'Yes of course,' she said rather sullenly and walked in.

Mother was finding it difficult to remove the earthquake newspaper from her head. It had planted a doubt. She had made a mistake, it was telling her. She should never have agreed to the eighth floor. Too high, too high . . . 'The builder did say he has put in earthquake-resistant structures, right?' mother asked.

I had to distract her, take her mind away from whatever was brewing in her chest. One major issue still needed to be resolved, and could just about work as a distraction. Ora had been left behind in the Guptanagar house. We thought at that point that she was too old to be trained to live in a flat where there would be a garden only on a leash. And she would have to learn to shit in a sandbox.

'Do you think she can manage that?' I asked.

'What?' mother asked.

'To shit in a sandbox . . .' I said.

'I don't know . . . I don't think so . . .' Ora was used to defecating in the large garden in the Guptanagar house. With great difficulty she had been trained as a puppy not to defecate in the house. If we brought her to the flat, she would have to learn to wait till she was taken out on a leash, or she would have to defecate in a small corner of the house. It was a complex matter and it helped to shift the conversation from the earthquake newspaper.

That would be an effective way of keeping doubt from creeping into mother's mind, I thought. Each time she talks of the earthquake and whether we had made the right decision, I will talk about Ora, I told myself. That would keep her occupied for the first few days.

The tactic failed in a matter of hours. Later that night, mother walked into my room as I was making desperate attempts to sleep. The room did not carry the fragrance of familiarity. The ceiling fan did not make the same rattling sound. Crickets did not play their symphony as they did in the fields outside my window in Guptanagar. And mother went on to make matters worse. 'We did the right thing, no Robin?' she asked sitting down on the edge of my bed.

'Mother, please . . .' I finally said, exasperated. 'You are the one who was stuck in Guptanagar all these months. You are the one who had the Six o'clock Syndrome problems. You know exactly how dangerous that place is. You know exactly what happened to Geetaben. You are the one who pushed to move out. And now you are asking me if we did the right thing?'

'Doubt is a natural thing,' mother said patiently. 'Don't shout like this. Gives a bad impression to the neighbours . . .'

'And what were you going to do if I said that we did the wrong thing?' I said unable to control my temper. 'Pack your bags and go back to Guptanagar?'

'Good night, Robin,' mother said in a hurt voice and walked out of the room.

We found out later that our improvised blessing for the mezuzah, born out of manipulating the blessing for lighting Shabbat lights, was almost exactly as it should be said. A Hasid with his flowing sideburns who knew the prayer book by rote would have been proud of our invention.

*Barukh atah Adonai, Elohaynu, melekh ha-olam
asher keedishanu b'meetzvotav v'tzeevanu leek'boa
mezuzah*

Blessed are You, Lord, our God, King of the universe,
who has sanctified us with His commandments,
and commanded us to affix a mezuzah.

God should be pleased, I thought.

CHAPTER TWENTY-ONE

Ora was sitting tethered to a stool in the kitchen of the Guptanagar home, her eyes looking sad and imploring, when mother walked in a couple of days later. Ora had rushed out of the house when the maids had momentarily left the garden door open after we packed and left. A stray had almost bitten her, and since then she had been kept tethered in the kitchen. Her only human contact came during the two meals she was fed.

When mother saw Ora, the dog could barely breathe. Her leash was a labyrinth around the legs of the stool, giving her no room to move. Her frustrated tug-of-war had entangled her even more, and the leash was pulling at her throat.

Mother had scolded the maids for not caring for her beloved Ora. But she knew that she could not completely depend on the maids to provide the dog with human company. They could feed her, but they could not become her friend like mother was.

All the same, a new set of rules was given to the maids: give the dog company, sit with her for a while, let her run freely in the garden at least for an hour every day and, at all costs, keep the garden door closed.

That evening mother sobbed at the dining table of the new house as we sat down for dinner. 'She is not a dog any more. She is my only companion,' she told me. 'We can't do this to her . . . Isolate her like this. She has become human after all these years. You should have seen her face when I left today. I have never seen her so quiet.'

'What do you suggest we do?' I asked. 'She has been wild all her life chasing sparrows and hunting baby squirrels and crows. Do you think she can live on the eighth floor?'

'No, but we can at least try. We haven't even tried. You know she has been indoors since the riots . . . It has given her some training to live without the garden. And anyway, she is growing old. She doesn't need to run around so much.'

That night mother woke me up around 1 a.m. 'We have to get Ora here,' she told me with urgency in her voice.

'It's one in the morning, mother . . . Can't we do this later?'

'Look, either you are coming or I am going on my own.'

So in the middle of the night we walked half an hour, found ourselves an autorickshaw, rode to the Guptanagar home, put Ora in the rickshaw and, for the first time, brought her to the flat. With Ora the last of our possessions had now left Guptanagar. It was empty, down to the bone.

Although I was irritated with mother for the midnight sortie, I understood the deep bond she and the dog shared. The story goes back ten years, when Ora was part of a litter of five and the wildest among the lot, destroying anything she could lay her paws on. She was born in the year the Babri Masjid was brought down and 'demolition' was her middle name. Anything that her newly acquired teeth could grab was chewed to bits.

Mother was away in France on a writer-in-residence programme for three months during that time. My friend Amit and I had been locked in by the curfew, and thought we could not have done a smarter thing than getting a pup to keep us occupied. During a break in the curfew we rushed in a rickshaw and brought her home from the house of a classmate where she was born.

And that is how Ora, the cobra-fighter and pigeon-eater, entered our home. But very soon I realized that she was an unmanageable pup, not the kind that would gently lick your face and listen to your every command. She would defecate and urinate in such unexpected corners of the house that I would realize she had done so only when it began to stink badly. I would come home from college after the curfew had been lifted to find her sitting proudly on the divan in the living room, having chewed out a large hole in the bed sheet. All that remained of my precious Israeli sandals were shreds of leather. If I tried to spank her, she would bare her sharp, little teeth and snap.

That was also the time when Manali, whose mushy poetry had fallen out of the drawers during the earthquake, was part of my life. Manali had ebony black skin, eyes that were even darker, a thin waist and large breasts that I liked to fondle. About sex she had one very strict rule—no penetration, no intercourse, only foreplay. Intercourse was directly related to marriage. Virginity had to be zealously preserved for the man who would marry her. Virginity had to be lost on a bed of rose petals after the legal document of marriage had been signed. Like in the movies.

So we rubbed our sweaty bodies over each other with our underwear on and faked orgasms. But even this act would fill her with guilt once in a while. She would cry, 'What am I doing? Why do we have to do all this . . .'

She was looking for divinity in love, and divinity, at least according to her definition, did not include any form of sex—with or without underwear. Sex contaminated love with a strangely addictive drug. Her upbringing had taught her that all things addictive were morally bad.

I would try and circumvent the underwear fortress by claiming that sex or whatever we were doing was nothing but a physical expression of our affection for each other. That 'all this' was natural and driven by instinct and that one can't feel guilty for something as primeval and innate as instinct.

The underwear fortress would still not be breached as we moaned and groaned over each other. I was getting increasingly frustrated with what the family later termed as 'chaddi sex' but I would not tell Manali about the lack of pleasure. Apart from these half-hearted sexual escapades, I cared for her and knew that the guilt of intercourse would be unmanageable for her.

But 'innate instinct' did not understand terms like 'caring' and 'affection'. Unable to free itself from the confines of two pairs of underwear, innate instinct turned into an ugly knot of anger in my groin. It started travelling through my body to my head and manifested itself in severe beatings for Ora. I would walk into the house, step splash into a puddle of her pee and, in a fit of mad rage, catch her by the neck and vigorously rub her nose into the puddle. I would be sitting on the Freudian couch strumming the guitar. Ora would be nestled behind me. Only after I had finished playing *Norwegian Wood* would I realize that she had chewed off a large part of my new kurta. The result would be a spanking on the flanks and the nose. I would hold her small body down and hit her till she stopped bristling and gave out a cry of pain. I would not feel satisfied until there was total submission. The knot of anger would be released only by the painful whining of the dog. Remorse was out of question. Groin anger did not have room for remorse.

This went on for more than a month until the very sight of me would make Ora cringe. If I called her she would come to me with her tail between her legs. It was the sort of power I would not unleash on Manali. I would not pull her underwear down and thrust myself in to douse the fire in my groin. I would not do that. I would beat Ora instead.

When mother returned from France she was surprised to find a dog that crawled and whimpered every time someone called out to her. Even if mother raised her hand to clip her hair, the dog would cringe. Raising a hand only meant one thing for Ora—a beating. 'Has someone been beating this dog?' mother immediately asked me. 'This dog has lost her spirit. She has been crushed.'

At first I did not confess to the crime, but soon I did. I had to. The evidence was all there. I was the crusher of a wild and free spirit.

Mother took it upon herself to cure the cringing. She would spend hours with Ora in her lap, constantly caressing her white coat. If Ora did something that I would have considered unacceptable, she would look sheepish and scared, expecting a beating. But mother would not hit her, and she had already barred me from giving any further spankings. Instead, she would pat her on her back and gently say, 'No.'

As repentance, I spent time with her in the garden chasing squirrels and letting her playfully snap at my hand. It took nearly a year, but she finally stopped cringing and lost her fear of beatings. In the process mother and Ora became inseparable. It was a bond that would only be strengthened by her cobra-fighting skills and her ability to sit quietly by mother's side while the world around them throbbed with an uncontrollable frenzy of violence. This bond was so strong that she would realize that mother was going out of the house the moment she put on perfume. She would keep staring at mother with her ears pushed back as if saying, 'Please don't go . . .'

Although it wasn't always obvious, her wild side too had returned. Carcasses of pigeons, doves and baby squirrels lying in pools of blood would be found in the garden regularly. By the way she sat on my stomach every evening licking her paws, while I watched television, no one could have guessed that Ora was the hunter.

It was this wild hunter that mother and I were afraid would not fit into the flat—a place high above any garden, where there were no snakes to fend off, no doves to hunt. And how would we teach her to defecate in a sandbox now that we had given up on beating her?

Mother and I had sat down one day before shifting and decided that it would be impossible to keep a dog on the eighth floor. Who would take her down when she wanted to urinate and defecate, who would toilet train a ten-year-old dog, where would we keep her when guests came, would she learn not to run out each time the door opened? These questions had seemed unanswerable at that point. We had only two options. Either we give her the injection and put her to sleep, as the euphemism goes, or we give her away to someone who had a garden and would like to have a good watchdog. Both of us were against the fatal injection. We did not have the stomach to watch her die, and we would not let her die in the presence of strangers. We would give her away, it was decided.

But dogs past their prime are not exotic emu eggs that everyone wants. Many of the old family friends who had learnt to keep pets from Dada were contacted. All refused with a plethora of excuses, and we had no option but to leave her in the abandoned Guptanagar house, needing a midnight sortie to bring her to the flat.

Mother thought she would be relieved by Ora's presence in the new home. She was wrong. On the couple of occasions that she tried to take her for a walk stray dogs chased them. Mother had a hard time keeping the strays at bay and controlling Ora who, in a state of panic, wrestled hard to free herself from the leash. They would both return exhausted and extremely worried. If Ora could not be taken for walks without attracting the strays, they were in trouble.

In the flat, Ora developed an unnerving habit. She would sit in front of mother and stare at her with her ears pushed back for hours. 'What is wrong with this dog?' mother would say, slightly irritated. If she walked into the kitchen, the dog would follow her. If she went into the living room, the dog would still be behind her, staring all the time.

Ora's behaviour could have been interpreted in many different ways, but mother felt the dog was trying to tell her that she had made a mistake. It was too much for mother. She needed to be told that shifting to a new house was the best thing that could ever have happened to the David family. She needed that assurance, but Ora did not have the capacity to lie for the sake of false assurances. She could only stare, which in turn heightened the doubt in mother's head.

And so, after all the turmoil, Ora was taken back to the Guptanagar home.

Help came from Piloo Framji, a senior member of one of the oldest Parsi families of Ahmedabad, and a friend from Dada's time. He had initially refused to take Ora in spite of having a large garden. He was tired of caring for dogs. In fact he had put to sleep his two Doberman Pinschers just the year before and did not want the burden of another dog, no matter how small.

But he called up a couple of days after Ora had been sent back to Guptanagar. 'Your father just told me that I should help you,' he told mother.

'I see,' mother said and chuckled.

'No really,' he said seriously. 'I was getting down from the staircase, looked into the garden and saw this plant of wild orange flowers swaying in the wind. You know who had given me that plant? Dada of course . . . It seemed as if Dada was trying to tell me through the flowers that I should help you.'

Mother was hoping that he would keep Ora himself, but he found another Parsi family in the old city of Ahmedabad who had a garden and many dogs.

For the next few nights mother and I slept badly. We would wake up every morning in a collective bad mood, and keep a safe distance from each other to avoid flare-ups.

Questions were eating away at my soul. Questions that bother me even today.

When I think of Ora, I think of myself. I think of the anger and the violence stored in me. If I can hit an animal so severely that it cringes at my very sight, what does it say about me? How different am I from Ahmedabad's mobs of rioters who were hoping to hit the other community so hard that it would cringe. So that it would fold its hands and beg, 'Please, we will do anything you say . . .' Could my violent temper be compared to the violence in the city?

Ora would die two years later in the Parsi gentleman's loving lap. Would she have preferred to die in mother's lap? Or in my lap, perhaps? There is no way of knowing.

CHAPTER TWENTY-TWO

It rained all night one week after Ora was given away. And for the first time we slept through the first shower of monsoon, completely unaware of it. On the eighth floor, we could not hear the sheets of water hitting the earth. With two more floors above us, we could not even catch its pitter-patter on the roof. For some strange reason, we even slept through the thunder and the lightning. Nothing woke us up to this shower of silence. We had come closer to the clouds and yet we had moved away from the rain.

Only in the morning did we realize that the air was misty, a curtain falling silently all around us.

'Can you smell the earth?' mother asked as we stood in the balcony watching the rain and sipping tea.

'No,' I said. I was missing the fragrance of wet earth. I could imagine it sculpting invisible pillars of scent around the Guptanagar house. In fact in Guptanagar the earth seemed to give out the moist fragrance even before the first shower. Along with the croaking of frogs in the neighbouring fields and the mating of the geckos in the living room, this fragrance was a sign that the monsoon had arrived.

Besides, whatever little sound the rain made was drowned in the morning sounds that only flats can make—the crushing of spices in a steel pestle, wet clothes being incessantly slammed with a small wooden bat, carpenters hammering furniture in the flat right above ours, the sweeper knocking at 7 a.m. for the garbage bin, women talking to each other by shouting across balconies, pressure cookers whistling, Hindi film songs blaring on the radio. All these were alien to us, since we had lived for nearly twenty years enveloped in birdcalls and barking dogs and the rumble of water tankers and earthquakes. And more recently, the bursting of crude bombs and the deathly silence of curfews.

'Strange, isn't it?' mother said.

'What?' I asked.

'All the sounds that flats can make and all the sounds they can't make . . .'

'Yes,' I agreed.

'You can't even see the moon from our balcony.'

What did the moon have to do with the sound of rain? I said nothing fearing that mother would start listing the defects of the new house. Where would we go from here if this house was flawed and Guptanagar was dangerous?

'It rises and sets behind our flat, and I never get to see it,' mother was talking about the moon. In Guptanagar, on the other hand, we only had to come out into the balcony to bathe in celestial light on full moon nights. We could sit on the terrace and imagine the world as a throbbing canvas in dark blue.

In the new house the same moon had been reduced to a diluted white glow on the top right-hand corner of the flats. The glow confirmed that the moon was there, somewhere behind us, but it was not possible to see it.

All the same, I was not ready to criticize my new house after signing on loan papers of more than seven lakh rupees. The amount was big enough to remove any possible defects. With mother, however, it was different. If and when she wanted to, she could look at such issues without attaching a monetary angle to them. I was hoping she would stop drawing out this list of defects and showing them to me, so that I would start regretting the decision to move to the eighth floor, start regretting the fact that we could not smell the rain or see the moon.

So I said nothing, hoping she would distract herself. Instead she took her complaint to a higher level.

'You know in the afternoons after you leave, it is so silent . . . Even a curfew is not so silent.'

'How do you mean?' I could not believe that our home, our abode of perfect safety, of perfect sanity, away from the madness, could be compared to the curfew.

'I can't explain it. You have to stay here to experience it. There is not a sound, especially after noon. You know the birds filled in the silence in Guptanagar. Their chirping and fighting for scraps, and the attack of the mynahs on our kitchen window and Ora barking her life out chasing squirrels and sparrows . . . But here, you can't hear anything.'

I continued to stare at the rain.

Mother remained quiet for a while and then said, 'Of course there is the odd call of the peacock and the kite screeching, but that's it. After that everything becomes so still . . . I don't know what happens. I suppose all the men go to work and all the women who don't go to work go to sleep. But it is worse than the curfew. Of course there are the carpenters just above us hammering away, but in all this silence, the hammering only drills holes into my head . . .'

I was not sure if this was a criticism or a mere observation. If it was criticism, I knew where she was taking the discussion: towards finding a justifiable excuse to return to Guptanagar. I remained quiet, staring at the rain and its shower of silence.

Mother said after a while, 'I have to tell you something Robin, but please don't lose your temper. It is important that you try and understand.'

I said nothing.

'You won't lose your temper?'

I shook my head to indicate that I would not.

'I was standing in the balcony the other day in the afternoon and a strange feeling came over me. A sort of strange dizziness. I can't explain it. I started feeling dizzy and then I wanted to jump down . . .'

'What?'

'I felt like flinging myself down. Just jump down, then and there . . . As if some strong force was nudging me to jump. I had to pull myself away from the balcony and sit down in the living room.' Mother kept looking at me, waiting for a response.

'Mom, we are not going back to Guptanagar and that is final . . .' I said firmly.

'Look, this is not about going back. It is about me doing something very stupid. Something dangerous. I am afraid of myself . . .'

'Has this happened only once or . . .?'

'It has happened more than once. That is one reason why you will never find me standing in the balcony by myself. I have stopped going there in the afternoons. I think we need curtains . . .'

'And what do you think triggers this . . . this desire to fling yourself?' I asked, still not sure if she truly felt this strange sensation or if it was a mere excuse.

'I think I have developed a fear of heights. Some kind of vertigo or something . . .'

'This is the limit, mother,' I was not able to keep my resolution to not lose my temper. 'If you want to go back to Guptanagar, just say it. Don't give me all these long-winded excuses. I mean you have never mentioned fear of heights in the last thirty years. And then in less than a month of shifting to the eighth floor, you suddenly develop a fear of heights? Please mother, this is too much for me to handle . . .'

'Don't insult me, Robin . . .' she said in a hurt voice. 'It is something I can't control. It is out of my hands. And don't raise your voice like this. People can hear you here. This is not Guptanagar.'

'So what do you suggest we do? You know I don't have the powers to turn the eighth floor into the ground floor.'

'I mean, you know . . . we still haven't sold off the Guptanagar house. We still have that.'

'Do you think this fear of falling is some sort of throwback of the earthquake? You think of the tremors when you stand in the balcony so you feel dizzy and feel as if you will jump down involuntarily . . .'

'Why can't you believe that it can be some kind of physiological condition I can't control? Do you think I am mad? Do you think I don't understand the magnitude of the entire act of shifting? You are not the one who had to live through a curfew hour after hour, day after day. It was me. It was my hell, that Guptanagar house.'

'Then why do you want to go back to it?'

Mother said nothing as she stood fidgeting.

'I suspect you have become used to that hell. You feel comfortable in it.'

'This is ridiculous, Robin. This is . . .'

'No mother, what *you* are saying is ridiculous. After taking this massive loan, after giving away more than half the things in the house, after shifting the entire house, you now want to go back to Guptanagar. This is absolutely beyond me.'

'Robin, you have to understand. It is not in my hands.'

'And what will you do if something happens during the rath yatra?'

'I can be here on the day of the rath yatra and then go back.'

'Mother, do you seriously believe that something can happen only on the day of the rath yatra? What if something starts before, or even after, the yatra? Then what am I supposed to do? Leave everything and rush off to rescue you?'

'Okay, okay. I know how to take care of myself . . .'

That was the first major argument we had in the new house, at the end of which mother finally decided she would not go back until the rath yatra was over. Once it passed peacefully, she would be free to do what she wanted. I also told her bluntly that I would not return with her. That she would have to learn to live alone, with me visiting her once in a while.

But by then the wheels of mother's return had been set into motion. I confess that there were brief moments when I too was drawn to the Guptanagar house. As if we were being pushed into returning by a force beyond our control. As if the Guptanagar house had turned into an empty void—a black hole that was pulling at us, drawing us out of our new home and laughing all the time. As if it was saying, 'You think you can live without me? I will see how . . .'

I fought the force, but mother gave in. Even the mezuzah, as I would later argue with mother, did not have the power to stop her. Because it did not have the power to stop the fear of disasters from entering homes. Whether it can stop entire disasters from entering is still a debate in the David family, but its ineffectiveness to ward off the fear of disasters is not an issue any more. It can't.

The astrologers of Ahmedabad confirmed this. The local newspapers were agog with their predictions of another major earthquake within a couple of weeks of our settling into our new home.

'It's coming soon, aunty,' said Seema Patel, our perky young neighbour. 'It's coming soon . . .' She was standing in the kitchen-side balcony of the flat below us and chatting with the rest of the flat owners, when she noticed mother, drying clothes on the plastic line.

'What is coming?' asked mother, not having read the Gujarati newspapers.

'The earthquake. Haven't you read the papers? Next Saturday, the astrologer said.'

'What are you talking about?'

'Arre aunty, this one astrologer I have been reading about says it's on Saturday. The next big earthquake. That is the day it will strike . . . And you know why I believe him?' she asked mother without expecting an answer. 'Because he has never been wrong in the past. He had even predicted the last earthquake . . . You know, the major one last year on Republic Day? That one . . .'

Mother listened to Seemaben's earthquake talk because she could not cup her ears and shout, 'Please shut up!' to a neighbour she had only recently befriended. Just as she would not sit under a tamarind tree for fear of the witches that hung upside down—fear dating from her childhood—even though she did not believe in witches, she did not want to ignore the words of the astrologers even if she did not believe in predictions.

'Tell us if you feel anything,' Seemaben added, as if she had not caused enough damage already. 'After all, you are on the eighth floor . . .'

'Yes, and if we die we will all die together, right?' mother said, and walked back into the flat, leaving the neighbours to laugh sheepishly.

Mother was afraid to use this as an excuse to convince me to return to the Guptanagar house. The last argument over her desire to jump off the balcony was still fresh in her mind.

But then something else happened. Seemaben came up for a cup of evening tea a couple of days later and casually talked about a conversation that she had overheard between schoolboys playing cricket in the parking lot. 'Is that a Parsi couple next door to you? I hardly get to see them. They come late at night, leave early morning.'

'Yes,' said mother. 'Sweet couple.'

'And they have put the picture of a bearded man on their door . . .'

'Zoroaster. It is their prophet.'

'I noticed you have also nailed something on your door.'

'Yes, a mezuzah it is called. It is considered auspicious in our religion to have it on the entrance of your home. All Jewish homes have it. Signifies the presence of God.'

'You know the boys playing downstairs? They said something so strange . . . They said two Muslim families had come to stay on the eighth floor.'

Mother was shocked. 'Why would they say something like that?'

'Because the thing on your door has characters that look like Arabic and the Parsi prophet has a beard. They said he looked Muslim.'

'So all bearded men are Muslims and all writing that looks unfamiliar is Arabic?'

'No, of course not . . . These boys, you know, they don't understand anything.'

'And what if Muslim families come to stay on the eighth floor? Does it have to become a subject of discussion?'

'No, aunty, that I can understand. Who wants to live with Muslims? And that too in a time like this? Isn't that why you left your old home? To get away from Muslims.'

'Frankly, I don't know what we were running away from. But tell me, what is wrong with having Muslim neighbours?'

'See, what if someone tries to burn their house? Wouldn't the flames burn our house too? Besides, I don't know why, I am just not comfortable living with Muslims. They are not our type. They are not like you and me.'

The conversation would turn out to be the last straw for mother, who was already finding the fear of falling too hard to handle. That night when I returned home mother was sitting on the Freudian couch with her runaway bag from the time of the earthquake resting on her lap. She had made up her mind to return. I screamed, threw things around the house, but it did not help. She would leave and not return.

It was only much later, after mother had shifted back to Guptanagar and I had claimed the main bedroom in the new house as mine, that we discussed what went wrong that night. Mother told me about Seemaben and the boys who saw us as Muslims and left me in a state of shock. I had understood then that for some of these youngsters, who had never lived a riot or walked a curfew-bound street, there were only two kinds of signs that made up this world: Hindu signs and Muslim signs. There were only two kinds of people that inhabited their world—Hindus and Muslims. All that was not obviously Hindu had to be Muslim and therefore bad. If I said that the boys had divided their world into good Hindus and bad Muslims, it would be an exaggeration. But it would be fair to say that they had a generalized and rigid definition of a Muslim, a definition that was unlikely to change as the boys lived in that part of the city where few Muslims ventured. Where contact with the 'other' would always remain limited to reinforce stereotypes.

'I felt as if there was no difference,' mother had said. 'Whether I was in Guptanagar or in some posh part of the city where there were no curfews, it made no difference. People said and felt the same things. The same anger and the same hatred and the same unexplained fear. They just put on better clothes and talked in a refined accent, that's all.

Guptanagar is better. At least I don't feel like flinging myself down eight floors here.'

Two years after the riots, mother had started feeling a numbing pain in her right ear. Loss of blood circulation to that ear, the doctor told her. 'Like a twin-engine plane,' he had said when I inquired. 'If one engine stops receiving fuel, it will lead to loss of balance.'

'Is there a name for this . . . this condition? Like vertigo or something?' I asked.

'No name. Bad body postures can affect our vertebrae, which in turn can affect blood circulation. Happens sometimes.'

'But can it lead to dizziness while looking down from a height? Can it lead to some kind of fear of heights?'

'Not impossible.'

Mother had been right. Her fear of falling was beyond her control.

■

On 13 July 2002 the *Times of India* hailed the peaceful passing of the rath yatra as a 'triumph of peace amid unprecedented stringent security arrangements'. The details:

> As predicted, the procession was not as thickly attended as in the previous years—40,000 compared to the two lakh of 2001—and was marked by heavy police and paramilitary presence: 30,000 security personnel including the BSF, CRPF and other paramilitary forces. The chariots in Ahmedabad were escorted by

commandos and bomb disposal squads. Choppers conducted aerial surveys repeatedly over the sensitive areas, much to the wonder and amusement of residents. The rath yatra was also under the constant surveillance of the chief minister's security adviser who monitored the yatra over telephone thirty kilometres from the Jagannath temple. The route was also restricted to a kilometre from the usual three kilometres. But this did not in any way diminish the religious fervour.

So effective were the security measures taken that the only incidents that took place were two minor stampedes in Shahpur Adda, a Muslim majority area.

'Residents of the minority community' observed a 'janta curfew' and advanced their Friday afternoon prayer timings. Leaders of the community had advised their people to go to the mosques near their homes. The entire route had been sanitized earlier on account of the terrorist threats and the recent communal tension in areas where the procession was to pass through the day.

Two days later, it was reported that while peace prevailed in the entire state, central Gujarat had been witness to communal flare-ups on the day of the Jagannath rath yatra, as the 'two communities' were engaged in pitched battles on the night of the yatra in Kheda and Petlad towns. The situation continued to be tense the next day and curfew continued in Kheda.

CHAPTER TWENTY-THREE

What you give away, you should never be made to regret. But we were soon to regret it all. Had we known that mother would return to the Guptanagar house so soon, we would not have gifted away half the things we did. Like Dada's wall clocks. Or the emu eggs. Or framed photographs of Dada standing next to Jawaharlal Nehru, taken when Nehru visited the Ahmedabad zoo and Dada had escorted him around. There were also the capital seats, which mother had arranged one above the other to construct a small pillar in the garden and placed a cement tank filled with water on it. It allowed the birds and the squirrels to bathe without worrying about Ora. These were beautiful objects. They had been part of the family. They were us. And now they were part of someone else's family.

Mother did get some of the objects back even if it put her in an awkward position. For instance, she got back a cupboard full of animal books gifted to a private library. She also got back some of the antiques from Dada's time.

But she was not able to get two fragments of her life that had disappeared. There was Ora, who the Parsi family refused to return when mother contacted them. 'No . . . please . . .' they told mother, 'we have fallen in love with her. We will die without her.'

'I too will die without her . . .' mother had argued, but they held on to Ora and we never saw her again.

There was also a small marble chip no bigger than a foot long. It was an ordinary piece of smooth marble that we had considered entirely giveable when a family friend asked for it. Mother had given it away with just the flick of the wrist and a casual glance.

But now she missed it. 'Water bounced off it and caught the morning sunlight when I watered the garden,' she told me. 'It had a strange transparent quality. Almost spiritual . . .'

Mother and I believe that the desperate bid to leave the Guptanagar house before the rath yatra had made us blind. Beautiful objects we would otherwise have clung on to for dear life, we were ready to give away eagerly. It was a sort of temporary insanity in which we trusted old acquaintances we would never have trusted without the backdrop of the rath yatra.

For instance, we trusted a family friend while disposing of the antiques and artefacts. He said he did not understand how to evaluate old objects and sent an art collector instead. The collector insisted that most of the artefacts were either cheap replicas or of low quality. He also said he had no money and sent an art dealer instead. The dealer offered a price. Mother accepted.

Later, through another acquaintance, we found out that all the objects had been repaired and polished and now adorned the farmhouse of the art collector. We are told he flaunts the collection as priceless. 'I wonder if every possible person lied to me . . . maybe they were all hand in glove,' mother told me when she found out. 'How they must be laughing behind my back. I hate this feeling of being cheated.'

'When you give away something, it ceases to exist for you,' I told mother. That is how I dealt with giving away.

Mother and I also believe that until the riots our Guptanagar house had been as exotic as the human child marinated in formalin. It shocked and amazed visitors. It was easy to tell that they had never seen a house like that before. They carried it in their heads and talked about it to their friends. And we liked that. We liked the fact that our house had no replica. It was custom-made to our needs. Without these shock objects, the house looked barren. Just like our new house, where there were forty other houses in our tower and they were all identical.

After mother returned to the Guptanagar house she coined a new 'syndrome' for herself on the lines of the Six o'clock Syndrome—it was christened the Lonely Child Syndrome and involved this giving and wanting back. 'As the only child, I was possessive about everything around me,' she told me. 'I hated to share. But Dada and your grandmother insisted that I learn to share, learn to give. Everything had to be shared with friends, cousins . . . Or you would be taken on a guilt trip. So I gave. And then I regretted giving and I wanted everything back. But it is not that simple now, is it? It is not that simple.'

CHAPTER TWENTY-FOUR

I wanted to run down eight floors and climb seven floors again to tell my neighbour in the opposite block that I hadn't actually been staring into his home. Yes, I had been staring from my living room on the eighth floor into his living room on the seventh floor, but that was not to nibble at his private life. It was just that the cable operator had not yet connected our television, and the final of the Natwest trophy was on between India and England. Yuvraj Singh, the stylish left-hand batsman, and Mohammed Kaif were playing what commentators like to call the 'innings of their lives'. Loud cheers were welling up from the many living rooms in front of me to signify that India was winning. And I was being left out of the festivities, for the first time in what was now my home, without a cable connection and without mother.

Because everyone in that seventh-floor flat had their heads turned towards the television set, I had assumed that they would not notice me peeping from a distance at the fuzzy outline of Yuvraj Singh gracefully drawing invisible straight lines hitting fours and sixes.

Obviously one of them must have noticed my rather large body resting on the Freudian couch with my head turned towards them. After a while, just when I had turned my head away for a moment, one of them got up and gently pulled an off-white curtain in front of my eyes.

I was hurt, even guilty. But I would not go across and apologize much as I may have wanted to. I did not wish to start a new life as a peeping Tom. If the word spread, and in flats the word can spread faster than in isolated bungalows, I would be doomed. 'Isn't he the fellow who was peeping into Mr So-and-so's house the other day?' neighbours would ask each other each time I walked out of the house, I feared. And once that happened, I would lose the opportunity to peep into nothing less than sixteen balconies and through them into sixteen living rooms in the opposite block. And of course a part of the bedrooms as well through the large glass windows.

'Maybe I should go and apologize,' I told myself, but how could I apologize to a complete stranger, living fifty feet away, for peeping? What if it was mere coincidence? They may have pulled the curtains without noticing me. What if they opened the door and screamed at me, 'Go away you dirty animal!'? What if they simply refused to admit that they had seen me sprawled on the couch when I would be able to tell from their eyes that they had?

Besides, is it really true that I don't like to observe other people's private lives? The fact was that I loved it. I was excited about having sixteen balconies in front of me. For the first time I had been given the opportunity to look at other people's homes and their lives simply by standing in the balcony of my new home. It was as if I had sixteen television sets in front of me, each with a reality show on. People trapped in small cases, their facades of strength starting to fade, their weaknesses and quirks becoming more evident, their fights and their moments of intimacies all revealed.

It was just a matter of making my large body less conspicuous. Perhaps I could turn off the lights and stand in the living room, a little away from the balcony. That would make me invisible. The problem was that the further I stood from the balcony the fewer balconies I could observe. Only six in fact, instead of sixteen. I could try switching off all the lights in the house, but even that would not work. The lights from the sixteen balconies gave out enough illumination for people to be able to make out that there was a silhouette of a man standing there, hunched with his elbows resting on the railings, head protruding and eyes voraciously swallowing neighbourly privacy. Peeping Tom. Dangerous.

But the fear of being labelled a peeping Tom was nothing compared to the pleasure of peeping. I had stolen too many glances already and the bug had bitten. Tired men in tired banians sitting on cheap wooden furniture and watching Anna Kournikova and her taut body glide energetically on the trimmed grass of Wimbledon. Her glistening, white, muscular thighs, her thick, golden braid waving excitement into uneventful lives.

Down below, a woman comes out and stands in the balcony in her flowing tent-like nightgown. Her husband joins her, the drawstring hanging limp from his pyjama. Both stare at the traffic in the lane next to the apartment house. They exchange a few quiet words and then the husband goes back in. At no point during their brief time together does either of them show any sign of affection, no gentle caress of the cheek, no attempt to hold the other person's hand. Not even a gentle pat on the back to signify friendship. As if all that had to be said and done had already been said and done. As if they knew that the other person was going to be there forever. Certitude.

Above the Kournikova-gliding-on-trimmed-grass home there lived another family with an old lady, most probably the grandmother, who often sat quietly in the balcony till late at night. She never switched on the light in the balcony. All I could tell from the silhouette was that she was aged, fat, wore her sari in the Gujarati style and sat on a low stool. And she looked straight into my flat, into the sixteen balconies above and below me. Sometimes she sat there endlessly, unflinching, unmoving. Was she staring into my home? My life?

In all my voyeuristic observations the one fact that intrigued me the most was that none of the sixteen balconies ever projected a burst of emotion. I never saw a father slap his son for misbehaving, or a daughter swearing at her mother for interfering in her love life, or a husband push his wife against the wall in a moment of passion. Not even the deep-throated laughter of drunken men over a dirty joke.

All I came across were men and women walking languidly between rooms, men watching television, boys working on computers with one eye on the television, women dusting the furniture . . . Life just went on a fixed routine. Like a constant drumbeat that never changed, never wavered. The drum player never seemed to miss a beat or lose his concentration. As if in a trance. Forever.

I believe that I was intrigued by this even drumbeat, this

non-violent, non-passionate routine, because it was in complete contrast to our Guptanagar home. There, if anything, a new drum player arrived almost every day, and played his own version of the rhythm.

For instance, there was the drunk who carried his bile-like home-brewed liquor in a plastic bag and generally swallowed it in one gulp. He would then start his volley of obscenities, with *'Thhari maane maro lund dau'* (Let me give my penis to your mother) being the most common. The expletive would be flung at anyone who came in his way, until the bile liquor started travelling through him. His curses would then be reduced to someone striking the drum set with a brush at the end of a darkened alley, the brushings only just audible in the darkness.

Then there were the women from the neighbourhood slum who would regularly start a shouting match on who had first rights to using the public water tap, the only source of water for more than 500 huts around. They would shout at each other continuously, not waiting for the other person to finish her argument—an electric guitarist competing with a trumpeter for speed at the cost of melody, both forgetting they are playing a duet.

There was also the mad rumble of the water tankers from the neighbourhood businessman's borewell, who made a living out of selling water. He kept a variety of vehicles to vend water. The roll of the large lorries, for instance, resembled 500 pianists slamming uncontrollably at the bass keys all at the same time. The smaller lorries resembled forty first-time students in a trombone class, all trying to play one clear note till their last breath would break.

There were of course other instances that could be set to a rhythm but I choose not to. Take the case of the father who had many years ago stripped his teenage daughter in public because she had eloped with a Muslim boy; or the farmhand who hanged himself because his neighbour's daughter—the object of his desire—was about to marry someone else; or the group of teenage boys who nearly got beaten up by a group of angry Rabari men for teasing a girl who was part of a marriage party. Or take the loud fights that emanated from inside our house. All this I will pass over perhaps because I don't know which rhythms to set them to.

What mother and I did not realize was that these rhythms, these drumbeats, were mere accompaniments to the singular constant drone humming away day and night without being noticed by anyone. It was a tanpura being played for so long it was a given. You had to make a special effort to pick it out and listen to it. Like you have to make a special effort to listen to the wind. Obviously we were not paying attention. If we had, we would have heard the hum of the growing hatred between the two communities above the din.

Had we heard this hum, this drone, it is likely that we would have left our home much earlier and escaped the burning of the shops, the blast of the crude bombs, the rattle of rusted metal swords, the stoning of the seventy-year-old rickshaw driver, the stripping and the murder of Geetaben and above all the unbearable silence of the curfew.

I am still amazed at how easily we had chosen to ignore this drone of hatred. How easily it had merged into the silent nights to give an impression of normalcy and permanence. How we thought it was silence when it was not.

In the new home the only objects that screamed, that brought out wild mood swings, drunken love songs and ferocious foreplay all around me, were the television sets in other people's homes. As if it was the soul of these homes that projected quiet exteriors. Because there had to be something going on in these homes. Because when people live together, they fight, love, have sex, scream at the servant, shout at the milkman, argue with the man delivering groceries at their doorstep. Why was I missing out on the action? Or did these people really live such uneventful lives? Did this routine not change even during the violent outbursts of the riots, while Geetaben was being stripped and murdered, while I walked on curfew-bound streets, fearing for violent mobs and my circumcised penis?

Behind curtains, it must be there that the eventful things happen. In the land where everyone can peep into everyone else's house, emotional outbursts are things you hide. Behind curtains you can do what you want, but your neighbour should not come to know of it. Your neighbour should only see a dull, uneventful picture.

But there came a time when I too needed to hide behind curtains. I walked out of the bathroom and into the bedroom one day, stark naked, wiping myself pleasurably and listening to Thelonious Monk belt out melody. It was only after a while that I realized I had turned into a peep show. Without a single curtain on any of the windows, people from the same balconies that I spied on could get a full view of my large, uneven body moving from one room to another, shaking to music they could not hear. Within two days I had large, white curtains put on all the windows including the sliding glass door in the balcony. The peep show was over. Both for me and for my neighbours.

You might think I don't like my new house, but let me say that there are many advantages to being on the eighth floor. You may not be able to hear the rain fall, you may not be able to smell the earth, but at the same time the mounds of dust that rise with the wind on summer afternoons do not make it to the eighth floor in as much quantity as they do in Guptanagar. You can leave the windows wide open at night without fearing for the tenacious battalion of mosquitoes singling out exposed flesh. And when there are no mosquitoes, there are no geckos chasing each other's tails. Also, you many not be able to see the moon on full moon nights, but neither can the sun cook the house into a radiation chamber.

Besides, everything is new. There are no cracks on the walls that Dada may have failed to repair and remove. There are no drawers filled with the forgotten poetry of past girlfriends. And the walls don't carry objects from three generations back. In fact I have hung nothing on the walls. I like them bare. I like to think that I have the power to decide what will hang on them. I like that.

Acknowledgements

This book would not have been possible without the unflinching support of my family—my mother Esther, my sister Amrita and my brother-in-law Nathaniel. They stood by me through my moments of self-doubt, never letting my spirits fall. I am thankful to my friend Anita Vachharajani, who went through the manuscript with a fine-tooth comb and helped give the book shape. I am thankful to Krishan Chopra of Penguin India, for his faith in me. I am also thankful to Jaideep Bose, Executive Editor, *Times of India*, and Bharat Desai, Resident Editor, *Times of India*, Ahmedabad, for allowing me to write the book. The final touches to the book were given by Jaishree Ram Mohan, for which I am most grateful.